THE LEARNING BOOK
THE BEST HOMESCHOOL STUDY TIPS,
TRICKS AND SKILLS

David L. Farmer, B.S., M.Ed.

Strategic Book Publishing
New York, New York

Strategic Book Publishing
An imprint of AEG Publishing Group
845 Third Avenue, 6th Floor - 6016
New York, NY 10022
www.StrategicBookPublishing.com

ISBN 978-1-60860-734-1

Printed in the United States of America

Book Design: Linda W. Rigsbee

DEDICATION

For my family,
who have taught me much more than I have taught them.

TABLE OF CONTENTS

INTRODUCTION

This is a book for homeschool students and teachers. It is a "How To" book about the best study techniques.

I have written it because when I began my teaching career, I was perplexed that many obviously intelligent students often earned poor grades while other students with less ability would receive excellent grades. As a result of this apparent anomaly, I began a life-long investigation into how we learn. I have spent years experimenting on my students with various techniques to see what worked and what did not.

During the course of my study, I noticed that even though the principles of learning are universal over all cultures and times, nearly all of what had been published was directed at traditional school students and was often slightly oriented to getting better grades rather than actual learning. The books, of course, contain much valuable information on learning, but also discuss how to be noticed by the teacher and how to bargain for better grades. These may be valuable strategies for traditional schools, but are more psychological/social behavior than learning skills.

Most books on learning techniques, because they are directed toward traditional students, fail to address the uniqueness of the homeschool experience. Most homeschool teachers are also the parents of their students, and I believe are more interested in having their students know the best ways to actually learn data and skills rather than knowing where to sit. Let's face it, when there are only three or four students in the class and the teacher is your parent, there isn't a whole lot of psychological value in sitting where you will be noticed. (And you can't even sit in the back and slouch down if you don't want to be noticed!)

Homeschools are uniquely different from traditional schools in several areas. Most often because of the biological relationship of teachers and students, the teachers know their students' strengths and weaknesses and can tailor courses of study and activities accordingly. Another difference is the tremendous variety in the structure of homeschools. In fact, there is almost as much variation in homeschools as there is in the personalities and philosophies of the families involved. Homeschools, too, have greater flexibility in scheduling class time. The parent, as teacher, is often the best judge of what the student needs at any given time and has the option to change the schedule on very short notice, or actually with no notice at all.

I believed that because homeschools are so unique, their students should have a guide to study techniques that work best in their environment. In this book, I am giving students the essence of what I have learned over the years about the best study techniques and presenting them for the home school environment.

Finally, psychology defines learning as any relatively permanent change in behavior that can be attributed to experience. The dictionary defines it as an acquired knowledge or skill. When I refer to learning in this text, I mean knowledge or skills that have not only been acquired, but also retained in whole or substantive part for a relatively long period of time or until needed. It is this learning I want to help the student accomplish.

Students will not use every technique in this book, but mastering and using just some of them will help to develop more effective study habits. So, it's OK to pick and choose, to discover how that particular technique fits into the overall scheme of learning. Use what works for you.

Sir Francis Bacon said, "Some books are to be tasted, others to be swallowed, and some few to be chewed and digested." I think that The Learning Book is a book that you can taste, swallow or digest.

I hope this book will help you to accomplish your educational goals.

Learn well.

"They know enough who know how to learn."
Henry Adams

CHAPTER 1

THE LEARNING BOOK: THE BEST HOMESCHOOL STUDY TIPS, TRICKS AND SKILLS

How would you like to study less and learn more? Dumb question, huh? That would mean you could get better grades on tests. It would mean you wouldn't have to work as hard. And it would mean you could have more free time to do what you want to do. The principles of how to learn effectively and quickly are well known. Unfortunately, they aren't taught very often in public, private or homeschools.

Being homeschooled gives you some unique advantages. First, your parents care enough to have made a decision and a commitment to homeschool you. Second, your schedule is more flexible than if you were in a more structured school environment. Third, you may have a bit more freedom in what you study. To help you get the most out of your education, this book will show you the best study skills, techniques and shortcuts so that you can study less, learn more and retain that information longer.

So, let's get started!

BUILDING THE FOUNDATION FOR LEARNING

We can learn all kinds of tricks and little shortcuts that will help us to study less and learn more. However, to get the most mileage from this book and from your innate skills, we must first look at a firm foundation on which to build those skills and the techniques that we will explore later. The stronger we build the foundation, the larger the building can be. Here are some of the basics to understand before we look at more specific learning techniques.

✦ TIP #1
Understand what motivation really is, intrinsic vs. extrinsic.

Why do we do the things we do? What makes us strive to win a race, choose a dessert, lift weights, learn to knit–or study? In a word, it is *motivation*. Motivation is what "moves" us to do a particular thing. When I was in high school, I heard a psychologist say something that caught my attention.

He said, "Everything we do consciously, we choose to do."

Being a slick high school senior, I disagreed, of course. I told him, "I certainly would rather work on my car or watch television than study algebra."

He wisely pointed out, "That's what you think you would rather do, but what you really want to do is study algebra."

I thought this guy had exceeded the stupidity limit. I told him, "No way. Not algebra–cars and television!"

Then he asked me, "What will happen if you don't study algebra?"

I told him, "Well, I will fail the algebra course."

"And then what?"

"I will be grounded."

"And then what?"

"Oh, no car–no television."

I was beginning to see his point. I wanted (no, really, really needed) to pass algebra, or I wouldn't have a car to work on or be allowed to watch television–and it would really complicate my chances of getting into college. Did I really want to go to college? Yes–no–yes. Why was I "moved" to go to college? Because I wanted to have a good job, and I wanted to prove that I could get through college–no one in my family had to that point. Oh, and I wanted to learn. I wanted eventually to be able to fulfill whatever dreams I may have. So, motivation ultimately comes down to what we want for ourselves or for others.

Motivation comes in two flavors, inside (internal or intrinsic) and outside (external or extrinsic). If we want to do something because we really want to do it, then the motivation is intrinsic. It's what we want on the inside. If we really like learning algebra because we enjoy it, then the motivation is intrinsic. It comes from within us.

If we force ourselves to study because if we learn algebra, then we get a reward (or don't get punished–but that's negative motivation, which we try to avoid), then the motivation is extrinsic. It comes from outside us. It is perhaps what someone else wants for us, and we do it to please them rather than ourselves.

Which is better, intrinsic or extrinsic? I am very practical–I do whatever works. All things considered, probably intrinsic motivation is better. During the American Revolution, the colonists were, for the most part, intrinsically motivated by an idea to be independent from England. The Hessians were paid mercenaries, and their financial motivation was extrinsic. Who won? (By the way, after the end of the war many Hessians chose to stay in the fledgling United States, which offered more freedom and opportunity than their homeland. Hmmm, I guess then it became intrinsic motivation.)

For the purposes of this book, we have to assume that intrinsic is better. But, realistically, we don't always have intrinsic motivation. I did not develop intrinsic motivation for algebra until, as an adult, I needed to make some calculations for a building project I was planning. Guess where I went. I dug out an old algebra book to determine the procedure for finding the data I needed.

If you cannot find it in yourself to be intrinsically motivated to study a particular topic or subject, then extrinsic motivation is fine. Your parents can provide extrinsic motivation for you, or better yet, you may find a way to motivate yourself. For example, give yourself a reward when you learn the material or accomplish a goal.

✦ TIP #2:
Find out what your dominant learning style is and then play to that strength.

We learn in different ways. About 90% of us learn and remember most effectively by what we see. We are *visual* learners. Some of us learn better by what we hear. We are *auditory* learners. And some of us learn better by hands-on experiences, by manipulation. We learn through touch and doing. We are *tactile* learners.

It is important to realize that no one learns exclusively by any one learning style. We all learn by a combination of these styles, but for some of us one of these styles will be our preferred style, the style through which we learn best.

If you lean toward a particular learning style, I will indicate in this book when you may benefit from that particular learning style, be it visual, auditory or tactile.

VISUAL LEARNERS

Visual learners learn by seeing, reading, visualizing, watching and picturing information. They benefit from seeing information written or graphically illustrated, such as textbooks, outlines, illustrations, graphs, charts and pictures. All of us are visual learners, and for most of us this is our primary learning style.

Visual learners can be either verbal or non-verbal learners. The verbal learners benefit from reading and writing information. The non-verbal learners benefit more from seeing graphic information, such as pictures and graphs.

AUDITORY LEARNERS

Auditory learners are also verbal learners, but they learn best in a listening/speaking exchange. They learn most effectively when information is presented in a format using sound, such as lectures, audiotapes and discussions. They benefit from repeating out loud information to be learned.

Josh, who seems to have difficulty sticking with reading a textbook, but who is very comfortable in conversations with his peers, finds that he can become really involved in class discussions and lectures. He learns best by listening.

TACTILE LEARNERS

The tactile learner is also called the kinesthetic learner. *Kinesthetic* simply means to move. *Tactile* means to touch. These learners learn best when they are involved in hands-on activities. They learn by being in actual physical contact with what they are learning and by manipulating material, so they learn well from fieldtrips and lab projects.

For example, Jimmy, a seventeen-year-old with a canny ability to fix cars, finds reading and lectures of little help in his efforts to learn. But put him in a lab situation, and he can learn very quickly. He learns by actually working with the material.

✦TIP #3
Types of intelligence? Realize that there is more than one kind of smarts.

It's also important to know that there are many different kinds of intelligence. It is probably not accurate to define intelligence only by how well we learn academically in school subjects such as writing and math. I once had a student named Dale, who just couldn't write worth a darn, try though he may. He really struggled with any academic subject. But during a class discussion about trucks, the other students told me to ask Dale about his truck. Even though he wasn't too sharp in school subjects, as a high school senior he owned his own commercial cleaning business, had just bought a brand new pickup truck and was probably making more money than most of his teachers. Dale was learning in areas of intelligence many would not consider academic. But he was doing pretty well in his business, which he continued and expanded after high school.

You must decide where your skills and interests lie. If you are at high school level right now, you may be starting to think about your career choices. Some careers obviously will require college.

If you want to be a doctor or aeronautical engineer, please, go to college. (If you are my doctor, get a lot of education, please.) If your skills and interests lie more in a manual vocation, go for it.

None of this is to say that linguistic and mathematical skills are not important. They most certainly are important. But just realize that there are other areas of intelligence, such as how adept you are in music, mechanics, art, and even getting along with other people. Don't sell yourself short just because English or math is not your strongest suit. (But don't sell English and math short either!)

✦ TIP #4
Attitude counts. Basic to everything else in the learning process is your attitude.

Have you ever heard the saying: "If it is to be, it is up to me"? How about, "Give 110%"? Or, "When the going gets tough, the tough get going"? They may be overused expressions, clichés, but each has a soul of truth in it—as well as all those other motivational sayings that coaches use on their teams. That's why this same psychology is used in military, athletic and sales training. The essence of these sayings is to "Believe in yourself" and "You can do it." These motivational quips are used because, well, because they work.

Your parents have taken on a time-consuming and challenging labor of love in deciding to homeschool you. They are saying that they believe you are worth the effort and that you are very capable of succeeding in this enterprise. But in any teaching-learning situation, there are two sides. I have taught students who have gone on to Harvard—and many, with as much or more ability, who could have gone to Harvard. I have had students with all the ability in the world (well, almost–tons anyway) who have failed miserably and students with marginal ability who have earned A's for their work. What is the difference? It comes down to one word–ATTITUDE.

What is attitude? In aircraft, it refers to what direction the aircraft is pointing. In people, it refers to which way you are pointing–figuratively, anyway. It is how you see things: situations, yourself, your parents and other people. It is whether you see the glass as half full or half empty. Just like the kid who, when he finds a pile of manure, goes looking for the pony, it is you who determine where you are going and how you will end up. If you want to see the person who will determine your future, look in the mirror.

Do you have to have a can-do attitude? Well–yes. And a will-do attitude. The famous singer and actress Ethel Waters said, "I know I'm somebody because God don't make no junk." You have to realize who you are. You are special because there is only one of you. God didn't give you 100 billion brain cells just to go to the bathroom. You are a child of God, and God doesn't want His kids to fail. You have to believe in yourself and realize what potential you have.

Deuteronomy 2:12 says that you were created heads, not tails–winners, not losers. Do not sell yourself short. A lot of people believe in you. You are a promise and a possibility. Believe in yourself.

Attitude is sometimes very fragile and must be protected. In 1970, when Mel Fisher began searching for the lost treasure ship, the *Atocha*, he placed a plaque over his door that said "Today's the day." It hung there for 15 years, 5,479 days, while he spent millions of dollars and thousands of man-hours. Finally, on Memorial Day, 1985, that day was the day. That sign helped keep everyone's spirits up and their eyes on the goal.

The mind is sensitive to the information that enters into it. It makes no distinction as to whether that information is true or false. Because you can control what enters your mind, you can help maintain your positive attitude by screening out negative data. Allow only positive information to enter your mind. That includes what you read, what you see, and what you hear—not only what other people say, but what you say too.

Don't let anyone put negative ideas into your mind. Negative is not just what is untrue; it is that which unreasonably threatens your self-image and destroys your confidence. It's not negative if someone tells me that I can't carry a tune in a bucket. I know that my song bucket has lots of holes in it, but I don't dwell on it. (I just don't try to sing around other people.) I accept that fact and then play to my strengths. I'm still a nice guy, and there are many other things that I am good at.

Remember that your mind is not a garbage can with a hairy lid. Protect your mind and attitude and exercise some control over what goes into your mind. Feed your mind good stuff.

Part of your attitude is also believing in your ability. There is no question that you have the ability to learn because there's no way you could be dumb and still speak English, or any other language for that matter. You just have to learn to train your mind to be the efficient machine that God designed it to be.

CHAPTER 2

SET ATTAINABLE GOALS FOR YOURSELF—PLAN YOUR WORK AND WORK YOUR PLAN.

High achievers always set the goals they want to attain. Have you ever shot a .22 rifle, a bow and arrow, or thrown darts at a target? What would it be like if there were no target to aim at? Tough, huh? If you can't hit a target that isn't there, neither can you achieve a goal you don't have. Primary to all achievement is the need to know where you want to go. What would have happened to Columbus if he had set out without a compass or a destination? (We might be living in a land that hasn't been discovered yet!)

Conrad Hilton was the guy who developed the worldwide Hilton hotel chain. He started out small, but he had vision and goals. One of his goals was to someday own the famous Waldorf Astoria hotel in New York City. He placed a photograph of the Waldorf Astoria on his desk, even though he knew that its purchase was far beyond his reach. But, years later he was able to buy the Waldorf Astoria, fulfilling his dream of owning one of the most beautiful hotels in the world.

You must decide what material you want to master and to what degree you want to master it. Determine what you are willing to put into the task. How long are you going to study? When?

Where? How do you know when to stop studying?

Your goals are the targets you aim for. You may not reach all of them, or maybe not exactly when you want them, but there is value in striving for them. The poet Robert Browning said that "A man's reach should exceed his grasp, or what's a heaven for?" Reach for the stars, and if you only get a handful of stardust, well, that's more than most people have–and certainly more that you would have if you hadn't reached for the stars in the first place. This doesn't mean to be a pipe-dreamer, someone who only wishes and never performs. More people fail for lack of trying than fail because of trying too hard.

✦ TIP #5
Set different types of goals.

I once had the opportunity to interview an elderly gentleman, Benjamin, who had a unique story. As a young man still in high school, he made a list of one hundred things he wanted to accomplish in life. The list included not only what his career would be, the kind of spouse he wanted to marry and the lifestyle he wanted to have, but it also included other goals that were important to him, such as going as far north on the North American continent as possible and as far south on the South American continent as possible. It included living with the native Inuit of Alaska, with Native Americans, and running in a marathon. When I spoke to him, he had accomplished nearly all of his goals and at age 81 was still working on the remaining ones.

Most people never accomplish much because they never really set goals. For the most part, the only limitations you have are those you put on yourself. Your goals should include long-term goals, intermediate-term goals and short-term goals. Start with the big goals and then break them down so you can see daily progress.

Set your long-range goals first, your life goals. Now, if you are in eighth grade, for you, a long range goal may be to get to ninth grade. However, if you are in twelfth grade or in college, you may want to start thinking about where you want to go in life. Develop a plan. Carefully consider your future. What do you really want to accomplish in life? What do you want to be? What do you want to do? These long-term goals could include where you want to be in twenty to forty years. A pilot landing an airplane doesn't do it on the spur of the moment. He begins to set up his landing miles before he can even see the runway. But let's be realistic, if the next year or so is as far as you can plan—well, that's a start.

Intermediate-range goals should include what you must accomplish in the next five to ten years in order to accomplish your life goals. This could be college or technical school.

Short-term goals are what you should do within the next year. Break these down into what you should do this month, this week, today. There is an old saying that goes, "How do you eat an elephant?" The answer is one bite at a time. If you break your big goals down into smaller goals, the big goals will take care of themselves. I have found that people are the happiest when they are in the process of accomplishing a goal. This could be something as simple as your "To Do" list for tomorrow.

✦ TIP #6
Make your goals specific.

Remember Conrad Hilton, the man who developed the hotel

empire? He set a specific goal of one day owning the Waldorf Astoria in New York City. Have you ever heard anyone say, "Be careful what you wish for because you just might get it"? And that is talking about just wishing for something. What could happen when you actually plan to get something? It's not enough to say, "I want to get good grades." What grades? When? In which subject? Make your goals very specific.

✦ TIP #7
Write your goals down.

People who achieve have the habit of writing down their goals and reviewing them frequently. If you do not write down your goals, they aren't really goals at all. The most important thing you can do with goals, besides setting them, is to write them down and read them every day because this will keep your goals where they should be—out in front urging you on.

✦ TIP #8
Make a schedule for your goals.

Once you have set your goals and written them down, it's a good idea to put specific times on them. By what date do you want to achieve your individual goals? However, at the same time, keep in mind that your schedule for completing your goals should be a guide for you, not a straightjacket.

Actually, you can make a chart to write down your goals and to put dates on them. You work from the largest or farthest away and work down to the smaller, more immediate. When a farmer plows a furrow in his field and he wants a straight furrow, he doesn't look down at the ground in front of the tractor. He picks

out an object in the distance at the other end of the field and aims
for that. It's the same when you mow the grass—if you want
straight mow lines. If you aim at a goal in the future, it will be
much easier to stay on track now.

To make the chart, start with a calendar for the entire term.
Mark out by months and weeks, in as much detail as you can,
class time, field trips, etc. What do you want to have accomplished by the end of this school term? You may make as many
rows for goals to be accomplished as you need. This is your
master calendar. Keep it current.

YEARLY/MONTHLY GOAL CALENDAR

	Sept	Oct.	Nov.	Dec.	Jan.	Feb.	Mar.	Apr.	Ma	Jun
Goals										
Goals										
Goals										
Goals										
Goals										
Goals										
Goals										
Goals										
Goals										
Goals										
Goals										

Break the master calendar down into weekly calendars.

WEEKLY GOAL CALENDAR

September	Week One	Week Two	Week Three	Week Four
Goals				
Goals				
Goals				
Goals				
Goals				
Goals				
Goals				
Goals				

Then break your weekly calendar down into daily calendars. What must I do today?

DAILY GOAL CALENDAR

	Sun	Mon	Tues	Wed	Thurs	Fri	Sat
Goals							
Goals							
Goals							
Goals							
Goals							
Goals							
Goals							
Goals							
Goals							
Goals							

Now, keep this schedule where you can see it easily, maybe on the wall where you do your studying.

Also, keep in mind that time you choose to waste is not wasted time. By wasted time, I mean time that is not spent in recreation or contemplation–thinking–but time that is spent doing nothing because you plan to do nothing. Sometimes (sometimes!) we need this time just to clear our minds.

Sensory Learning Tips

Visual Learners: Keep your goal charts on the wall so you can see them all the time.

Auditory Learners: Read your goal charts every day.

Tactile Learners: As you read your goals, touch the calendar and the goals.

✦ TIP #9
Make your goals real and touchable whenever possible.

Keep your goals real and near. Look at them written down. Read them out loud. If the goals are material, get pictures of them. Keep the pictures where you can look at them every day. If possible, get an object that signifies your goals and touch that. If you can't touch the actual high powered telescope that you want, you can at least have the catalog with a nice picture and description near you. Whenever possible, touch your goals to make them more real to your mind.

We have found that most people are not motivated by the work they have to do, but by the rewards they can acquire by doing the work. So in sales training, we taught people to put pictures of their goals—new cars, new homes, nice vacations—where they could see them all the time, on their bathroom mirrors, on their desks, and on the sun visors in their cars. (One of our sales-training students, Michael, even wanted to put pictures on his rearview mirror because he didn't want to see where he had been, but where he was going. That's where we had to draw the line!)

These same principles will work for you. Most of us do not study simply for the sake of studying. We want the rewards that knowledge can give us, a good career, a secure future, and understanding. (Yeah, OK, also a nice car.) Keeping your goals real also means that if you know what you want to be, associate with someone in that career field. Want to be a doctor? Go to a hospital. Want to be an automotive technician? Go to a garage. See if you can shadow someone in that field for a day.

Sensory Learning Tips

Visual Learners: Write down your goals. See your goals. Post pictures of them. If you want to score 95% on the test, write it down: "I will score 95% on the vocabulary test." And keep it where you can see it all the time. See yourself in the college you want to attend. Visualize yourself graduating from that school and getting the job or starting the business you really want. If possible, get a picture of your goal and place it where you must look at it every day—on your desk, your bathroom mirror or how about the TV set (!).

Auditory Learners: Besides reading your goals out loud every day, record them on a tape recorder and listen to them.

Tactile Learners: Whenever possible, get close to your goals, so close that you can touch them. If you want to score 100% on the vocabulary test, make a perfect test for practice, then write "100%" at the top of the test and "Good Job!" (Don't forget that this is to motivate you to study so you can get the same grade on the real test–and don't forget to leave it behind when you are taking the real one.)

CHAPTER 3

HANDLING YOUR TIME WISELY

The most valuable asset you have is your time–and most people take time lightly. They waste it. And when it's gone, it's gone. You can never recover it. So the trick is to make the most of your time. By using your study time wisely, you can have more time for yourself.

✦ TIP: #10
Utilize time management and schedule your time intelligently by using a calendar.

The first step to using your time wisely is to find out just how you spend your time right now. The best way to do that is to make a calendar and do a time analysis. Here's how it works.

Make a chart for yourself similar to the one shown below. It should contain 24 hours a day for 7 days of a typical week. Block it out an hour at a time (some time-study experts suggest 15 minutes at a time). First, block in the time you spend in bed. Then block in the important time periods in the week–church, family events, meals (Don't forget food!). Block in your home-school hours. Put in your recreational time. Then see what free time you have left. Notice, I didn't say TV time. The average person watches 28 hours of TV a week and most of that is wasted time that you can never get back. Now, see what time you have available for study sessions.

CURRENT TIME USE CHART

	Sun	Mon	Tues	Wed	Thurs	Fri	Sat
6 AM							
7 AM							
8 AM							
9 AM							
10 AM							
11 AM							
12 AM							
1 PM							
2 PM							
3 PM							
4 PM							
5 pm							
6 PM							
7 PM							
8 PM							
9 PM							
10 PM							
11 PM							
12 PM							

✦ TIP# 11
Make your own study calendar.

Once you have seen where you are spending your time right now, maybe you will find that you already have adequate study time scheduled—or maybe you don't. Your study time should be separate from your "school" time, and the study periods should be relatively short with breaks in between.

Since you are being homeschooled, you probably have a little more flexibility in your scheduling. Your schedule should allow you to take a break after your regular class time. What study time works best for you, right after your regular class time (with that break in between, of course) or later in the day or evening? Whatever it is, schedule that time for your studying. Write it in your calendar. Then, stick to it. Probably, the best plan would be to study in blocks of one hour each, or less if you master the assigned material before the hour is out. And don't forget to include breaks every 15-20 minutes.

Now, make the same chart as your first time-study chart. This time make any adjustments to give yourself a regular study period.

PLANNED SCHEDULE WITH STUDY PERIODS

	Sun	Mon	Tues	Wed	Thurs	Fri	Sat
6 AM							
7 AM							
8 AM							
9 AM							
10 AM							
11 AM							
12 AM							
1 PM							
2 PM							
3 PM							
4 PM							
5 pm							
6 PM							
7 PM							
8 PM							
9 PM							
10 PM							
11 PM							
12 PM							

✦ TIP #12
Distinguish between class time and study time.

Just as if you were in a traditional school, there should be a definite time for class and then a separate time for studying. It's hard to actually learn new material while listening to a speaker or reading a book. Sure, you will pick up some of it, but to actually let the data sink in and be retained, you need multiple exposures over a period of time. A separate study time will help you psychologically to separate the class and studying. It also allows you to try out some of the techniques given here, and it helps the information you are trying to learn to gel in your Long Term Memory.

✦ TIP #13
Consistency! Be consistent in your study habits.

What kind of professional baseball player would practice only when he felt like it? Would you want to go to a doctor who only occasionally attended classes while in medical school? How about the pilot who skipped that part of flight instruction that dealt with landings? The same goes for you.

When I was a freshman in college, I had a friend named William, who had a very high IQ. Unfortunately for him, someone had told him what his IQ was. Because he knew he had tremendous native ability (That is, he was smart.), he chose to pretty much ignore the books and attend class only when he felt like it. As a result, he flunked out of college because of poor grades.

If you are going to learn something, then you have to stick to it. Be consistent in your study habits. Once you plan your study time, stay on schedule.

✦ TIP #14
Beginning is half done. Just get started!

You've probably heard this one. It's an old saying, and it's true. Once, I had the opportunity to work with a doctor on personal dynamics. He was very shy and we were helping him to have more confidence in dealing with people. His most difficult problem was his inability to call people on the telephone. He would do it if he had no other choice, but would most often let someone else handle his phone calls. What he discovered is that it's not so bad once he was on the phone. It was that initial dialing and waiting for someone to answer that bothered him. What was the root of his problem? I don't know. I'm not a psychologist. But once he realized that it was mainly starting the calls that gave him problems, with practice, it became much easier to make his phone calls himself.

It's the same for you. We can put off indefinitely what we don't want to do. We can find all kinds of excuses not to get started, when the only thing that really counts is actually getting started. Once you have started studying the subject, it isn't so bad. It's inertia. Sir Isaac Newton's laws of motion say that objects at rest tend to remain at rest and objects in motion tend to remain in motion. It's always harder to push a car from a dead stop than it is to keep it going once it is started. It works the same way for studying.

Try it. Force yourself to get started. Beginning is half done.

Sensory Learning Tips

Visual Learners: Start reading the notes.
Auditory Learners: Say it out loud: "I am starting now to…."
Tactile Learners: Pick up the book.

✦ TIP #15
Create your own study space

When you have a regular place to study, it's easier to get into a study mode. When you sit down at your desk, your subconscious knows why you are there—to study and learn. This is where you can keep your tools: textbooks, pens, pencils, paper, references books, and, if possible, a computer terminal. If it's in your room, fine. If it's a corner of the basement, that's fine too. Wherever it is, it should be some place that is your own and is accessible to your parents—for consultation, of course.

This doesn't mean that you are "hand-cuffed" to your desk. Sometimes it is good to take some of your studying, especially reading, to a new quiet location, just for variety. It is much nicer to read outside on a warm sunny day in May than to be inside the house reading.

TIP #16
You can increase your chances of learning data and concepts if you reduce interference when you are studying.

What is interference? Interference is anything that distracts you when you are seriously trying to concentrate. Did you ever have someone slam a door when you are watching a scary movie, or razz you when you are trying to hit a baseball? It interferes with your concentration and hinders your learning.

It will help if you have the same place to study each time. Being there will help put your mind in that "study mode." If soft music or Mozart helps to relax you, then by all means, play it softly in the background. Notice, I said softly in the background. If you need to concentrate on the music, go to a concert. Also, avoid loud or raucous music that makes you feel like you need to go out and hit something. Remember music is an aid, not the vehicle.

Sleeping right after you study will help to minimize interference. You remember better what you learned just before going to sleep. It's tough to study right up to bedtime, but try a brief review or recite a memorization or take a minute or two on a tough concept just before retiring. Often, when you concentrate on a problem before retiring, your mind will subconsciously continue to work on the problem while you sleep. Have you ever tried to recall the name of a person and then wake up in the middle of the night when it comes to you? That's your subconscious working for you.

Don't try to learn new material and review old material at the same time. It will create interference and confuse your mind. If you are going to review, review. If you are going to learn new material, then concentrate on that.

Sensory Learning Tips

Visual Learners: Avoid looking out the window while studying.

Auditory Learners: Try to keep your study area quiet, maybe with soft music playing in the background.

Tactile Learners: Try to handle only study related materials while studying.

✦ TIP #17
Make a "To Do" list.

People who value their time and want to make the most of it, often use "To Do" lists. I have done this for years. It is too easy to fritter away time without realizing where it goes. Then, at the end of the day, we ask ourselves what we have accomplished. We seem to have been busy all day, but just what did we get done? A "To Do" list will help you stay on task.

Every night before you go to bed, make a list on an index card of what you need to do the next day. Prioritize the list, putting the most important things at the top and the less important farther down the list. (When I taught my own kids this technique, they would write down, "1. Get out of bed. 2. Brush my teeth. 3. Eat breakfast." Sure, they got to cross it off their lists, but come on, you know you will do those things anyway.) When you wake up the next morning, you will already have your list of what you need to do.

CHAPTER 4

A LITTLE BIT ABOUT MEMORY

Most times when people have to learn something, they do it by rote memory, which is the hardest way to learn. That is, they just try to memorize it with very little knowledge of how to make learning it easier. Understanding how memory works and learning a few simple techniques will help you to learn and remember.

✦ TIP #18
Understand how your short term memory works

Your short term memory is similar to a desktop, like RAM on a computer.

Short term memory stores information for a while, several minutes perhaps. Think of being introduced to ten people at a party. How many names can you remember? Probably not many. That's because the information is stored in a temporary location with a limited amount of storage space. It's like having only one sheet of paper on which to write your life's story.

The short term memory is a filter, letting important data enter the long term memory. It filters out what your mind considers unimportant information and lets in what it considers important information. One of the techniques of learning is to know how to make your mind realize that the information you want to learn is important, a point we will elaborate on shortly.

✦ TIP #19
The more you know, the easier it is to learn: Long term memory

If short term memory is like a desktop, long term memory is like a filing cabinet or a hard drive. And it's a really big filing cabinet because there seems to be no limit to how much you can learn. It appears that the more you learn, the easier it is to learn even more. I once knew a minister who also had a medical degree and was at that time studying for his law degree. He spent most of his time in his study, uh, studying. (Well, maybe you can carry this study stuff too far.)

There are several factors that help to move information from your short term memory to your long term memory and make your mind realize it is important. One of those factors is repetition. The best way to remember someone's name is to repeat it out loud right when you are introduced. Hearing it out loud helps. Saying it out loud helps more. Saying it several times helps even more. Think about it. Try to relate it to something or someone else you know.

Another thing that will help you retain the information is if you make it even more important by concentrating on it. Consciously strive to imbed it in your mind.

Sensory Learning Tips
Visual Learners: Try to see the material in your mind's eye.

Auditory Learners: Listen to the material.

Tactile Learners: Write it down and shake hands with it (as well as with the person you just met).

✦ TIP #20:
Understand how we forget–and remember: the curve of forgetting

There is a concept in the study of memory called the curve of forgetting, which was first proposed by a German, Hermann Ebbinghaus, in the 1880's. It shows just how easily we forget things that our brain doesn't think important. Here is how the curve of forgetting works.

Let's say that you hear a one-hour talk on a given topic. If you do nothing with the material, when you walk away from that talk, you know 100% of whatever it is that you remember. You don't know all of the material that you heard, but you do know 100% of what you know at that point.

One day later, 24 hours, you will remember only 40-60% of what you knew when you left the talk. One week later you will remember only about 15-20% of the information, and by one month only 2%. And that's if you really paid attention. It's true that we have an almost unlimited capacity to learn new things, but we must get the material from our short term memory into our long-term memory. The way that happens is to make our minds realize that the material is important. If the mind doesn't see it come up again (or again and again), it will fall into the dark hole somewhere between our short-term memory and our long-term memory. How do we make it important?

One way to make information important and one of the main keys to remembering is to review! If you spend 10 minutes on day 2 reviewing the data, you will get your retention back up to nearly 100%. One week later, it takes only a five-minute review to get the retention back up to almost 100%. And after one month, only 2-4 minutes will bring up your retention to 50% to 90% of the original data. Only 50%? Come on. How much would you retain if you didn't review? Oh, only 2%. I'd say you are farther ahead to review. Just a couple of minutes a day review should be sufficient.

✦ TIP #21
Mnemonic devices and acronyms are mental tricks that you can use to help you remember.

Mnemonic means memory, and mnemonic devices are things that help us to remember. I can recall from eighth grade what the letters are on the spaces of a music scale: FACE. The lines are EGBDF. Now, with my musical ability, I have absolutely no idea of what that means. I can remember them because my eighth grade music teacher, Miss Germer, used mnemonic devices to help me remember. The spaces, of course, spell FACE. The lines are an acronym for "Every Good Boy Does Fine." EGBDF. What helped me remember was the acronym.

Acronyms are words formed by using the first letter (or sometimes letters) of words. FACE is an acronym. CARE stands for Combined Relief of Americans Everywhere. ZIP in ZIP Code stands for Zone Improvement Plan. You probably already know MDAS and ROY G. BIV. MDAS is the sequence for the order of mathematical calculations—My Dear Aunt Sally or Multiply, Divide, Add and Subtract. ROY G. BIV helps you to remember the colors of the spectrum, or rainbow—Red, Orange, Yellow, Green, Blue, Indigo, and Violet.

How about My Very Excellent Mom Just Served Us Nine Pizzas—the planets. Mercury, Venus, Earth, Mars, Jupiter, Saturn,

Uranus, Neptune, and Pluto (assuming that you still consider Pluto a planet. If not, it could be My Very Excellent Mom Just Served Us Noodles.). You can use this technique to remember items in a series. So, if you have to memorize a list, try making an acronym out of it.

✦ TIP #22
Alphabet Cues

Have you ever forgotten someone's name? A movie star? An old acquaintance? A recent introduction? Try using alphabet cueing. A cue is a suggestion, a hint. It's simple and, in fact, you may have already used it. Just start going through the alphabet slowly and see if a particular letter suggests the name that you are trying to recall. Chances of hitting the name are about 30-50%. But this isn't just for names. You can also use it to recall factual material. Even if you don't hit the right answer, let your subconscious work on it. Maybe you will wake up in the middle of the night again with the right name.

Sensory Learning Tips

Visual Learners: As you are going through the letters, try to see the name.

Auditory Learners: It may help to say the alphabet out loud. (If there is a crowd about, you may want to just whisper it. They may think you a bit odd.)

✦ TIP #23
There are many possible reasons for memory loss.

This is a book about learning and remembering, so we should discuss just a bit about memory loss. There are several causes of memory loss. That is, if we have really forgotten it after we have actually learned it. The most important cause is normal forgetting through unimportance, irrelevance or non-use (Remember the curve of forgetting?). But there could also be some medical reasons for forgetting easily: depression, stress, poor sleep, vitamin B12 deficiency or thyroid disease. If you find that you really, really have a hard time remembering material, you may want to have a check-up.

✦ TIP #24
Memorizing: Learn to train you memory to retain what you must memorize.

Henry Rutt used to be the Sunday School Superintendent at the small country church where I grew up. He was only 5' 2", but he was a big guy in a little body. The scripture and poems he memorized as a child were a comfort to him all his life. When he served with General George S. Patton as a chaplain's assistant during WWII and even later as a resident in a retirement home in his 90's, he could still recite the passages he learned as a child.

Some people have a misunderstanding of memorizing. They think that it is something that was done in the Victorian era as a dictatorial means of having people learn. Actually, much of what we learn starts as memorization: lists, sequences, poetry, prose and formulas, to name a few. It can also help us develop a feel for and appreciation of the English language. There is a lot of value in learning the Gettysburg Address or the Preamble to the Constitution of the United States.

Often, for me, passages of Shakespeare come to mind in different life situations. When I think of something that would be nice, I think of "'tis a consummation /Devoutly to be wished." Or something that is repulsive: "'tis an unweeded garden, /That grows to seed; things rank and gross in nature /Possess it merely," both quotes from *Hamlet*.

Why memorize? First, because it is a good mental discipline, exercise for your brain. It is flexing your mental muscles.

Second, because it helps to improve your self-esteem, knowing that you know a passage or data by heart.

Third, it's a good way to initially place material into your short-term memory in preparation for it to enter your long-term memory.

Fourth, it can really amaze your friends.

Usually, you can learn things that you like really fast. How about all those songs that you know by heart? Or what about those Shel Silverstein poems, from *Where the Sidewalk Ends* and *Light in the Attic*. This is all material that you will recall for years. So, you know that you can use memorization as a means to long-term learning.

Memorizing will always be beneficial to you, and this is a good time to practice and teach yourself how to memorize information that will be useful to you. Let's look at some of the best ways to help you memorize.

✦ TIP #25
Should you memorize in whole or in part?

It's best to memorize material as a whole whenever possible. If the material is really long, break it into several, shorter sections, but take the largest sections you can handle and then create a bridge from one section to the next. It will help to use 3x5 index cards here. Write down the material on the cards to carry them with you.

✦ TIP #26
Use the progressive part method.

The progressive part method is pretty simple. Learn the first section and recite it. Then learn the second section and recite both the first and second section. Then introduce the third section, etc., using short sessions and frequent reviews.

What you are doing here is memorizing sequentially. I used this technique to learn "Annabelle Lee" by Edgar Allen Poe. I did it in sections. It wasn't hard to learn the first four lines:

It was many and many a year ago,
  In a kingdom by the sea,
That a maiden there lived whom you may know
  By the name of Annabel Lee;–

After I had those four lines down, I tried the next two lines.

And this maiden she lived with no other thought
  Than to love and be loved by me.

Then I put all six together. I had the first stanza. Not so hard. I said it a couple of times until it began to gel in my mind.

Then I started on the second stanza doing it the same way. First, the first two lines without saying the first stanza:

She was a child and I was a child,

    In this kingdom by the sea,

Then the next two lines and repeated those four all together:

    But we loved with a love that was more than love—

    I and my Annabel Lee—

Finally, the last two lines and repeated the whole second stanza:

    With a love that the winged seraphs of heaven

    Coveted her and me.

Then I went back and said both the first and second stanzas a couple of times until I was sure I had them solidly in my mind. And I continued like this for each stanza. If you find yourself becoming fatigued, stop for a while and come back to it later.

✦ TIP #27
Build a bridge when you memorize in parts.

A bridge is a close association between two words so that when you say the one word, the other comes to mind. You condition your mind to recognize that one unrelated word can suggest another.

When I memorized the Dagger Speech from Shakespeare's *Macbeth*, I always had trouble when I came to the eighth line.

Is this a dagger which I see before me,

The handle toward my hand? Come, let me clutch thee:

I have thee not and yet I see thee still.

Art thou not, fatal vision, sensible

To feeling as to sight? Or art thou but

A dagger of the mind, a false creation,

Proceeding from the heat-oppressed brain?

And then I was stuck. There was no logical way to get from these lines to the next ones:

I see thee yet, in form as palpable
As this which now I draw.

So, what I did was to create a memory bridge from the last words of line eight (*"heat-oppressed brain"*) to the first words of line nine (*"I see thee yet..."*). The way to do that is to keep repeating the lines in succession and memorize the sounds of the words going together:

"heat-oppressed brain....I see thee yet,"
"heat-oppressed brain....I see thee yet,"
"heat-oppressed brain....I see thee yet,"
"heat-oppressed brain....I see thee yet,"
"heat-oppressed brain....I see thee yet,"
"heat-oppressed brain....I see thee yet,"

After doing that enough times to make the connection from *"heat-oppressed brain"* to *"I see thee yet,"* try saying it again, from the beginning. When you hear *"heat-oppressed brain,"* you should recall *"I see thee yet."*

Another way to make a memory bridge is to use the association of single words. In this case, repeat them in the same manner, but associate the word *"brain"* with the word *"I."* Keep making the *brain-I* association, until it is automatic.

"brain....I"
"brain....I"
"brain....I"
"brain....I"

When you come to *"brain,"* you should automatically think of the first word of the next line, *"I."* Also, you can use visualization here. Think of seeing a brain with an eye in the middle.

Sensory Learning Tips

Visual Learners: Concentrate on seeing the words on the paper and visualize them in your mind.

Tactile Learners: Listen carefully to the words as you say them. Try recording the passage and listening to it, then reciting along with the recording.

✦ TIP #28
Spaced repetition: Reviewing

Reviewing can be more helpful than many students think. You know that it is one of the key ways to move information from your short-term memory into your long-term memory, but did you know that the more you review, the less you have to review? Spaced repetition, or active recall, in the learning curve means that if you review frequently, the more time you can have between the reviews and the less time you need to spend on the reviews. Pretty good reason to start reviewing, huh?

✦ TIP #29
Form a memory chain to remember items in a list.

There are many different systems to improve your memory. The memory chain is a neat trick dating back to the time of the Greeks and Romans that will let you form associations between items to help link them together in a list.

Take several items on a grocery list, for instance. Let's say you have to go to the grocery store and pick up milk, eggs, hot dogs, soda, lettuce, paper towels, soap and flour. Here's what you can do to help you remember the items. I would picture a cow with a chicken on her back, eating a hot dog and drinking a soda. The cow is standing in a field of lettuce covered with flour. Beside them are paper towels and soap (to clean up with).

You can make your associations as goofy as you want. Sometimes, the sillier, the better. The important thing is that it helps you to remember the items.

✦ TIP #30:
Use a system for memorizing.

Memory systems may involve several techniques, but probably the most useful and easiest to use is a system that uses images to recall items in a sequence, for instance, a list of people. You can help improve your recall by using a system such as this. You assign a rhyming image to each of the numbers 0-10. Since it rhymes, it should be easy to remember. Once you have committed that to memory, use silly images to remember the names you need.

Here are some suggestions for the number system, but you can make up you own pictures, too.

0=hero
1=bun
2=shoe
3=bee
4=door
5=hive
6=sticks
7=heaven
8=bait
9=line
10=hen

For example, to learn the list of presidents, picture George Washington washing a bun (one) in his laundry tub. That's not so hard because everyone knows that Washington was the first president. How about the tenth president? That was John Tyler. Picture him tying up a hen from his chicken coop. Associate tying and hen–Tyler, #10. With some practice, this could make lists a little easier.

✦ TIP #31
Use mental pictures.

It is easier to remember pictures than words, so whenever possible, turn the information to be learned into vivid, even bizarre pictures. You could picture William the Conqueror landing at Hastings in 1066 as actually landing in an airplane with the number 1066 on the tail of the plane. You could picture Mesopotamia as a messy place after a dinner where you could get ptomaine poisoning (food poisoning).

Sensory Learning Tips

Visual Learners: Actually visualizing mental pictures should help you remember.

Auditory Learners: Talk to yourself about it. Tell a story about it to help you remember.

Tactile Learners: Try drawing an actual picture of a scene incorporating what you want to remember.

✦ TIP #32
Make things meaningful by making them familiar.

Do whatever you can to make data meaningful. It is the best way to move data from your short-term memory to your long-term memory. I used it when learning the nonsense poem "Jabberwocky" by Lewis Carrol. Even if you have never heard of "Jabberwocky," it's a fun poem. It starts out like this:

T'was brillig, and the slithy toves
Did gyre and gimble in the wabe:
All mimsy were the borogoves,
And the mome raths outgrabe.

Do you wonder why it's called a nonsense poem? To help me remember it, I related *"brillig"* to *thrilling* and *"slithy toves"* to *sliding loaves*. Use whatever works.

When I was a kid, I had difficulty with *stalactite* and *stalagmite*. I couldn't keep straight which was which. Then I used the association that in order to hang from the roof of a cave, it had to be tight—stalac-tight. I had the same problem with *longitude* and *latitude*. So I associated longitude, running north and south with the line plunging down—plunge-itude.

Sometimes the more bizarre the associations you make, the easier they are to remember, like seeing a brain with an eye in the middle of it.

If you don't completely understand something, assign it meanings. For instance. think of what a pronoun is. *Pro* means *for*. So, a *pro-noun* is a word that stands for a *noun*, like *he* for *James* or *her* for *Susan*.

✦ TIP #33
Elaboration will help you remember.

We have been talking about the process of elaboration throughout this book, we just haven't called it that—yet. Elaboration is taking information and turning it over, looking at it in different ways, chewing it up a bit and seeing how it tastes. Summarizing, paraphrasing, asking and answering questions, using mnemonics and forming mental pictures are all kinds of elaboration. *Elaborate*, as a verb, means to work out in detail. The more different ways we handle information, the more familiar we become with it and the better we can remember it.

✦ TIP #34
Take a mental walk.

Associate what you want to learn with a trip that you take regularly, such as to church or a friend's house. Then, assign what you want to learn to various landmarks along the way. Let's use the grocery list analogy again. Here are the items we must remember: milk, eggs, hot dogs, soda, lettuce, paper towels, soap and flour.

As you leave, picture a cow and chicken standing there waving good-bye to you. Next, you stop at the stop sign, and standing there is a hot dog drinking a soda. Farther down the road is a traffic light made from a head of lettuce on top of a roll of paper towels. Finally, as you pass the firehouse, you see a flower taking a bath with a bar of soap.

You can make your trip as short or as long as whatever list you need to remember.

Sensory Learning Tips

Visual Learners: See it.

Auditory Learners: Say it out loud. Tell a story.

CHAPTER 5

STUDY TECHNIQUES FOR EFFICIENCY AND EFFECTIVENESS

We have discussed some foundations for studying more efficiently and a bit about memory. Now let's get down to more specifics.

✦ TIP #35
Discipline is a good thing. Make it work for you.

Ever wonder where the word *discipline* comes from? I didn't think so. It sounds stern and scary, doesn't it? I once had a student tell me that she liked my class because there was no discipline in my classroom. I was surprised because I thought I had good discipline until I realized that she didn't understand what the word *discipline* means. I was always in control in my classroom and there was never any question of who the teacher was. She had confused the word *discipline* with *dictatorship*.

Here is what the word actually means. *Discipline* comes from *disciple* or *learner*, like the disciples of Jesus. For us it means someone who learns self-control or orderly conduct. It means training yourself to be in control of you, hence, a disciplined person. The subjects we study are also called disciplines. Our concern here is training, or disciplining, yourself to study. Sometimes we have others who are often older, wiser or more experienced than we are who help us develop skills and control. They are, technically, disciplinarians.

Discipline is often a factor of age and maturity. No one expects a five-year-old to have the same self-control (discipline) that an eighteen-year-old does. Be willing to accept discipline, instruction and advice from your parents. Remember that your parents have already gone through where you are now, and they have your best interest at heart. They probably understand more about you than you do about them.

The best discipline is intrinsic discipline developed by you from within yourself. Find a good role model, someone you really respect and want to be like, and pattern your life on that person's example.

✦ TIP #36
Study in short bursts.

It's easier to learn when you keep your study periods short. Most people can concentrate on a subject for about twenty minutes. After that, interest and concentration fall off significantly. A solution to this problem is to keep your study periods brief. It's a technique called Spaced Practice or Serial Position. What it means is that it's easier to remember things at the beginning and the end of a study period than in the middle of the study period. Even in lists, the easiest part to remember is the beginning. The second easiest part is the end. And the hardest part is the section right after the middle. So if the beginnings and endings are easiest to remember, increase the number of starts and stops. Instead of studying for 60 minutes, break it into three periods of 15 minutes each with a break of 5 minutes in between.

During your break, shift gears, do something different, even just getting up and walking around the room, but discipline yourself to get back to studying–right away.

Sensory Learning Tip

Tactile Learners: When you are taking the short break between study sessions and your body is stretching, you may want to mentally review *briefly* what you have studied.

✦ TIP #37
What are your biorhythms? Determine when you learn best.

Are you a morning person or an evening person? When do you function best? Do you jump out of bed in the morning ready to meet the world, or are you like me? I sort of roll out of bed, slowly. It takes me about one to two hours to hit my stride. However, in the evening, I can work up to and even past midnight if necessary, and still stay focused. (Just don't ask me anything important until after 9:00 o'clock the next morning.)

Keeping in mind when you feel most alert, try to schedule your study sessions when your powers of concentration are at their peak. If it's in the morning, try to get up a little early and get started right away. If it's in the afternoon, try to arrange your schedule to facilitate that time. And if it's in the evening, schedule your study time for then.

Also, you must consider that maybe you have no preference for any particular time of day. Then try to space out your study times to keep the sessions short.

✦ TIP #38
Make habits work for you.

Study every day. Review every day. Even if you are caught up on your work, take some time during your regular study period to do some reviewing. Bummer! Not really, the power of habits is amazing. Why does it always seem easier to create a bad habit than a good one? Bad ones just seem to creep in there, like watching too much television or chewing gum with your mouth open. Good ones require conscious effort, like brushing your teeth twice a day or hanging up your clothes.

It takes about 21 days to establish a new habit, either good or bad. Try implementing some of the suggestions in this book for 21 days in a row and see if it helps with your studying.

✦ TIP #39
Aromatherapy: Certain odors can help you relax, be stimulated or remember stuff. Cool, huh?

I have a friend in the restaurant business. He started by having a food stand at a local farm market. In order to draw in customers, he would set up a fan to blow the smell of his food toward the entrance of the market. You can easily figure out why he did this–to increase his business.

Did you also know that odors cannot only make you hungry, but also help stimulate your mind in several other areas? Aromatherapy is a science that endeavors to help us change our moods, relax or be stimulated by odors that we smell. Here are a few smells that may help you.

The fragrance of jasmine or peppermint increases alertness. Jasmine tea is a great pick-me-up. Try peppermint candy or chewing gum. It is also reputed to relieve headaches.

The smell of freshly brewed coffee is very stimulating, and green apple or cucumber reduce anxiety and help you relax. So does the smell of vanilla (It also makes a great ice cream!). Try washing your hands with green apple scented soap or shampoo and put a dab of it on a handkerchief or tissue to take with you.

Floral scents may improve memory. Sniff a floral scent when learning new material and again when you want to recall it. It is called state-dependent learning. Material to be recalled could be more accessible when you replicate that state in the future. Try putting a little on a cloth. But be careful because floral scents can also put you in a romantic mood! Maybe you better study alone if you use this one.

Sensory Learning Tip

This is pretty obvious. Although it does not fall into the categories of visual, auditory or kinesthetic, the olfactory sense (smell) is pretty powerful. Maybe you can use this unique technique to help you study—at least it could make you smell nice.

✦ TIP #40
Rewards: Make sure you reward yourself when you accomplish a goal.

You reward your dog when he does well, don't you? Why not reward yourself when you do well? The rewards don't have to be big ones—or expensive ones. If you like a special lunch, hold it off until after you reach a goal, maybe learning a selection of poetry or an algebraic equation, and don't you dare eat it until you have accomplished your goal.

Sensory Learning Tip

Tactile Learners: If you reward yourself with food, you may be a "taste learner!" Just make sure you don't reward yourself before you accomplish the goal.

✦ TIP #41
Say it out loud.

When you want to remember a name of someone you just met, say his or her name to yourself several times. It will help you remember the name. The same principle applies when you learn anything else. And when you say it out loud, think about it. Make it important. Try to lock it into your mind. Besides, the way you learn material is the way you will say it, so why learn it silently and then try to recite it out loud? Also, when you are saying it out loud, don't rush through it. Recite it at normal speed. The way you learn it is the way you will say it. I used to have students learn the National Anthem of the United States. I found that those who learned it by singing it to themselves, could only remember it by singing it again. Try writing it also because if you both say it and write it, you will retain the data much better.

Sensory Learning Tip

Even if you are a visual or tactile learner, use all of your senses to learn. Hearing yourself say it out loud will help. Remember, no one is exclusively a visual, auditory or tactile learner.

✦ TIP #42
Try to organize into logical chunks.

Since we have already talked about the Progressive Part Memorization method, this is a good time to apply the same technique to organizing data into chunks or blocks of information. Learning information in manageable chunks makes it easier to recall than trying to learn the whole thing all at once.

You know your phone number, don't you? Did you learn it as a series of ten digits, or as three, three and four? 717-555-1234. How about your social security number? That is three, two and four. 123-45-6789. It's much easier to learn material when you break down long bits of information into smaller segments.

✦ TIP #43
Since most forgetting occurs immediately after memorization, review frequently.

We discussed reviewing in our tips on memorization, but it is also valuable even when you are not trying to recall the exact words of a poem or numbers in a sequence. When you are reading, after a paragraph or two, review the material by jotting down the main points. After listening to a presentation, jot down or say out loud the main points. (Obviously, don't say them out loud if it will interrupt the speaker.) This will also help you focus and may suggest questions you might want to raise. If you are watching a DVD or listening to a CD or tape, stop it once in a while and repeat the main points, even if you have been taking notes all along. Reviewing, saying it out loud, writing it down—these all help to register the material in your long term memory.

Try reviewing old material just before you start studying new material, but be careful. Don't review old material and try to learn new material at the same time. The one tends to interfere with the other.

✦ TIP #44
Don't Go Hungry. Hunger impedes both learning and recall.

We learn better when we can't hear our stomachs growl, and we are not distracted by a conscious (or unconscious) hunger. So, if you need a snack before you study, OK. A snack! Not a banquet! That will impair learning and make you sleepy. Try to avoid sugary snacks, too. The more blood goes to your stomach to help you digest your food, the less blood goes to your brain.

✦ TIP #45
Knowledge of Results. You learn fastest when you have immediate feedback on your answers. Are they right or wrong?

It is best when you know right away if your answer to a question is right or wrong. This applies both to reviewing and to testing. Both are learning experiences. It's called knowledge of results.

There are several ways to get knowledge of results when you are studying. One is simply to close the book, ask yourself questions and then flip open the book to check the answer.

Another is to use 3x5 flashcards, index cards. When you know the answer on a card, place it a little way back in the pack. When it comes up again, place it a little farther back. When you know it three times in a row, place it at the back of the pack or put it in a separate pack to review later. Just before your test or quiz, review the entire pack.

Still another way is called Programmed Learning. Some books still use this technique, which was popular in the 1960's, where you are asked a question and then you turn the page to find if you have answered correctly. If your answer is correct, you proceed to the next question. If it is wrong, you are directed to another page explaining the correct answer. Today, computer learning programs use the same technique.

Sensory Learning Tips

Auditory Learners: Say the answers out loud. If your answer is incorrect, when you have the correct answer, say it out loud several times while thinking about it to implant it to your memory.

Tactile Learners: Use the index cards.

✦ TIP #46
Self-testing: Give yourself tests and quizzes on the material you have learned.

Since any involvement with material to be learned will help you assimilate and retain it, testing itself is a learning experience. In fact, just the act of making the test will help you learn. You can get Knowledge of Results, and see just how well you are doing, by giving yourself practice quizzes and tests. Make up some objective test questions: true-false, multiple choice, short answer. Let it sit for a day or two and then go back and take the test. After every question, check your answer. Chances are that many of the questions you choose to write will be the same as those your teacher would write.

Think of essay questions that may be asked of you. Make up more questions than you would have to answer on a test. Then outline your answers to the questions. Try to think like a teacher. (You might even want to try to trip yourself up by asking some trick questions. That should be interesting, especially if you really are tricked by your own questions!)

✦ TIP #47
Over-learning: Once you have learned the material, keep on studying!

Once you have learned material, continuing to work with it will result in further learning and help to solidify the material you have already learned. Study it more and over-learn it. You can do this by taking a break from the material you are learning and go to something else for a while, maybe even a day. Then come back and go over the old material. It will seem easier the second—and third—time than the first, and you will remember it easier. The better the material has been fixed in your memory, the longer you will recall it.

Sensory Learning Tip

Try using all your other senses here to over-learn, especially visual, auditory and tactile, but also smell and taste if possible.

✦ TIP #48
Go deeper into the material.

Once you have learned the material, not only continue to study it, but go into more detail about it. How does it work? What variants are there of it? How does it affect life and living?

As you review the material you already know, go more into depth on the subject, but only as much as your mind can absorb at one time. Remember that we said don't try to learn new material while reviewing old material. This situation will be a little different. In this case, you already know the old material well. The purpose here is to add depth and understanding to what you already know.

Try to use your other senses here too. If you are primarily a visual learner, try to use your auditory and tactile skills. Touch something. Listen to something.

Clint was a student of mine who so loved learning that he would consistently over-learn. If he were assigned an art project to draw a building showing perspective, while everyone else drew a building, he would draw a city. If the assignment were to learn thirty lines of "The Raven," he would learn all 105 lines. He became so good at learning that he eventually ended up on the TV quiz show *Jeopardy*.

If you are studying icebergs, you may delve deeper into different kinds of icebergs, effects of icebergs on shipping (q.v., *RMS Titanic*), or ecological effects of icebergs.

In psychology, the study of dyslexia may lead to finding out what famous people had dyslexia. For instance, Picasso, Edison, da Vinci, Alexander Graham Bell, and even Jay Leno and Henry Winkler, the "Fonz."

✦ TIP #49
Change focus for a while. Sometimes a change is as good as a break.

We can normally concentrate and absorb material for about 15-20 minutes. Then we need a break. Take a short one. This goes right along with studying in short sessions. During the break, take a short walk. Do something different to refresh your mind. Then when you come back to the material, do a brief review in your mind of what you had just covered before you start again.

Sometimes, switching to another form of study helps also. Move from studying material where you are sitting, to something where you are still in a learning mode but are standing or moving around.

Sensory Learning Tip

Tactile Learners: This is especially good for tactile learners. Moving and switching focus can help you concentrate. Sometimes just adjusting our posteriors in our chairs will help increase our attention span or intensify our concentration.

✦ TIP #50
Use short periods of non-productive time to study.

Ever think about just how much time you spend waiting in lines, waiting for someone else, riding in a car or bus or sitting in the bathroom? If you add it all up, we probably spend years waiting in lines, at red lights and in bathrooms. Wouldn't it be great if we could convert some of that time to productive study time? Always try to have a book or other study material with you to use during those down times. I have books in every bathroom in my house, on my desk and by my bed. I even have them in my cars, not to use when I am driving of course, but when I am stopped at red lights. I can look up now and then to see if the light has changed (And if I forget, the guy behind me will remind me.)

Keep some of your notes or anything else you want to memorize on index cards. They are easy to handle and fit in a pocket. When you are waiting at McDonald's to order your burger and fries, whip out the cards and do a short review.

✦ TIP #51
Use index cards.

I have mentioned index cards several times, so let's elaborate on that point. The 3x5 cards are a very convenient size to carry around. I almost always have a few stuck in my shirt pocket. I use them to make notes during the day on something I want to research, something I want to do or something that simply interests me. If I am learning a new language, I can keep some verb conjugations or nouns on the cards and take them out periodically throughout the day to review.

When I want to learn a poem, I put it on 3x5 cards and take them with me. When I have a bit of down time, I take out the cards and review them. It is great for vocabulary, spelling, foreign languages, formulas and objective material in general.

Sensory Learning Tips

Auditory Learners: If possible, say it out loud as you handle the cards.

Tactile Learners: Handling the cards while you study may help. It may also help if you make "doodles" that relate to the notes on the cards. You know, some kind of cartoon or drawing. This can give you a different visual perspective, and drawing them is fun.

✦ TIP #52
Use TV effectively: Avoid bad TV

Most television programming is mindless; and when you have finished watching it, you should ask for your time back. It contributes to being overweight and numbs our imagination. American kids watch an average of 28 hours of TV each week. That means that by age 65, that person has spent nine years in front of the tube. (Boy, how much could you learn if you put that time on math, writing or a foreign language?)

Avoid bad TV. What is bad TV? The easiest definition of bad TV is that TV which does not instruct, edify or entertain in a positive way. Programs that are filled with senseless profanity, violence and sex, either expressed or implied, cannot be a positive influence on our minds at any age. The cumulative effect of what we watch on TV must have an influence on our attitudes and our perception of reality. I don't have to see violence on TV to know that it exists in society. Besides, we learn better by doing a positive activity than by watching a negative one.

You can control what you put into your mind. Among computer programmers, there is an acronym, GIGO: Garbage In, Garbage Out. Your mind is the same way. You need to exercise discretion in what you choose to put into your mind.

✦ TIP #53
Utilize good TV.

If you have access to cable or satellite television, you have access to many good, educational channels. Many programs on TLC, Discovery, PBS, The Food Channel, The Disney Channel, The History Channel and A&E are excellent educationally, as well as entertaining. However, even with these networks, you still need to be discretionary. If your time is valuable, you don't want to waste it on junk.

Sensory Learning Tip

Both visual and auditory learners can benefit from good TV.

✦ TIP #54
Use Games. Help your brain with educational games.

One of the good things about games, besides being entertaining, is that they force us to think. The games that will benefit you the most are those games that force you not only to think, but also to think ahead and plan strategy. There used to be a popular puzzle called the "Fifteen Puzzle." It was plastic and had 15 moveable pieces that would slide around in a housing with 16 spaces. Normally, the pieces were numbered 1-15. The object of the game was to arrange the pieces in numerical sequence (after someone else had messed it up, of course). It was great fun and a substantial challenge for someone in fifth grade, which is when I had mine. I played with it endlessly, but once I discovered a couple of techniques to getting the numbers in sequence, it was no longer a challenge. Recently, I bought another one; and after a space of many, many years, I could still arrange the numbers very quickly. It felt great knowing that I could still do it, but the challenge was gone years ago. So I couldn't really exercise my brain with it any longer.

Many games can help you take a break from studying and still give your brain a workout. The best games for your mind are those that continue to provide challenges and entertainment, unlike the Fifteen Puzzle. To get good at them you have to strategize. Tick-tac-toe is obviously somewhat limited. With a reasonably skilled opponent, no one can win. Checkers is better. Chess is probably the best game for learning thinking and strategy skills. Word games, Scrabble, Blokus, Chinese Checkers, Jump-A-Peg, any game that forces you to think and reason can be beneficial. If you find that you have quickly mastered a game, it wasn't challenging enough for you. Pick a more difficult one.

Electronic games are fine, but pick positive ones. And don't limit yourself to only electronic games. The world is not virtual. It is real, and it's out there where you can actually touch things.

Sensory Learning Tip

Tactile Learners: Using games is a good way to learn planning and strategy skills.

✦ TIP #55
Learn how to handle frustration and stress.

Much of our lives is spent seeking that which comforts us and avoiding that which makes us uncomfortable and causes stress. Sometimes we refer to stress as worry or anxiety.

Everyone, at one time or another, is under some kind of stress, but stress is not always bad. Sometimes a little stress is good for us. It helps keep us sharp and alert, as we should be before and during a test. Too much stress is when our mind is distracted, when we worry about something, and when the stress keeps us from performing at our best. Stress can cause headaches, fatigue, emotional strain and even suppress our immune systems. It is for these reasons that we should have a way to handle stress.

If it's something you are worried about that is causing your stress, keep in mind that, by far, the vast majority of the things we worry about never happen. And the rest of them, we have little or no control over.

Here are some tips that may help you to manage stress, including some relaxation techniques.

1. When faced with a stressful situation, analyze the situation. Back off a little and look at the problem. Try to identify what it is that caused the stress? Why are you reacting the way you are? What should your reaction be? If you can do something positive to alleviate the problem, do it.

2. Exercise. Sometimes just moving your body helps to relieve stress. It could be playing a physically active game, jogging, or just going for a walk. Physical activity can release endorphins which are your body's way of easing anxiety.

3. Get outside with nature. Spending too much time inside the house even makes me depressed. Get outside at lease once a day. Enjoy the world God created for you.

4. Exercise your faith. Get closer to God. Maybe the best stress-reducer is your faith.

5. Look for good. Sometimes we are overwhelmed by what we construe as negative, by what other people say, by what other people do or even by watching news on TV. Stop for a minute and look for the good in all these situations. I have tried to live my life by a saying that I heard many years ago: "In the midst of every adversity, lie the seeds of an equal or greater benefit." What does that mean? No matter how bad a situation is, there is probably a bit of good in it somewhere—even though it may be pretty well hidden some times.

6. Get organized. Some people get flustered when they feel overwhelmed with work. Try taking a couple of minutes (well, maybe a little more than a couple) and organize what you have to do. Often, just making a list of what you have to do and prioritizing it will help you feel more in control. You still have as much to do as before, but now you are more on top of it.

7 Take a nap. Being tired certainly doesn't help stress. In fact, it causes stress. So, try a fifteen-minute nap. When you wake up, you may see the world differently.

8. Take a bubble bath or a shower. Yeah, right. Feeling good and relaxed can influence your mental attitude. Try it.

9. You might try deep breathing exercises to help you focus and get yourself together. Lie on your back or sit in a chair so that you are comfortable. Close your eyes and try to relax. Slowly breathe in and out. Listen to the sound of the air filling your lungs and listen as you slowly exhale, and try to feel the tension leaving as you breathe out. Do this for 10-15 minutes, and then lie quietly for another 10 minutes.

10. Meditation. Meditation isn't a bad thing, and it doesn't always mean transcendental meditation. (And it doesn't necessarily mean saying OOOMMM.) It is simply being in a quiet place, clearing your head and concentrating on peace and calm.

11 Talk to someone. Often, very often, it helps if you are stressed out to talk to someone else about it. Your parents, perhaps. If you feel you are too close to them, maybe your pastor or another person you trust. If you can, find someone who has already experienced whatever situation is confronting you.

✦ TIP #56
Use multiple sensory stimulation to help you learn.

If we can learn in three sensory ways, visual, auditory, tactile (seeing, hearing, touching), then try using all three to help you learn in three different ways. Say vocabulary words out loud. Handle note cards. Use self-talk. Use all of your senses, including smell and taste. If you are studying American history, check out some of Thomas Jefferson's favorite recipes and make them.

Sensory Learning Tip

Obviously, this is a "duh" tip. It's making good use of all your senses.

✦ TIP #57
Move and exercise to increase learning

Regular physical exercise offers a change from academic study, will help you keep your mind alert and active and help you learn. It could be an organized sport such as football, basketball or soccer, or it could be simply walking or playing pick-up games.

Regular physical activity supports learning and higher levels of self-esteem. Fitness levels and academic achievement are positively related. It's a fact—exercise helps keep your mind sharp.

Sensory Learning Tip

This isn't just for tactile learners. All learners can benefit from exercise.

✦ TIP #58
Get your weight on target.

Nearly one in six U.S. children is overweight. When we exercise and have our weight right, we feel better physically, we look better and we have better self-esteem. True, it takes a lot of willpower to turn down the ice cream and potato chips in favor of a salad or fruit. Most of losing weight is simply determining to do it, planning it and sticking to that plan. Of course, it's hard. That's why there are about a million diets on the market, and each one has the single best way to loose weight—easily. It will take some determination, but you can do it. If you find that there really is a problem, see a doctor.

✦ TIP #59
Understand whole vs. part learning.

We discussed whole vs. part learning earlier in the section on memorization, It's important to realize that whole vs. part learning applies to all of learning, not just memorizing. Whenever possible, learn material as whole unit. If the whole thing is too much, then break it down into manageable parts and learn each separately. Create a memory bridge between each part.

✦ TIP #60
To learn it, teach it. Try teaching someone else what you have learned.

Ask any teacher, and they will tell you that when they first started teaching, they learned most of the material the day before they had to teach it to their students. This is because when we teach a skill or a concept, we learn it better ourselves. And if we don't really know what we are talking about, it will become quickly apparent when we try to teach it to someone else.

Put yourself in the situation of having to teach a lesson in whatever it is that you are studying. If it is history, integrate as much information about that period or incident and organize it into a lesson to teach to one of your peers, or better yet, to your parents and a group of friends. Prepare the lesson and audio-visual props to go along with it.

Sensory Learning Tip

Teaching material that you are trying to master is an excellent opportunity to use all three of the primary sensory learning techniques—visual, auditory and tactile.

✦ TIP #61
Have charts and graphs around your study space, things that you make.

No matter what subject you are studying, make visuals for that subject. *You* make them. Don't buy one already printed by a commercial supplier. They may look better than yours, but you will learn more by making your own.

Make a list of irregular German verbs. Make your own periodic chart of the atoms. Make your own timeline of American History. Make a list of geometry theorems.

Sensory Learning Tip

Visual Learners: Place the visuals where you can see them easily.

Auditory Learners: Reinforce what you are doing by talking about it.

Tactile Learners: This is where you should shine. You are making the visuals, handling the visuals, and thinking about the visuals.

✦ TIP #62
Make history relevant.

Years ago when I started researching my own family history, I wasn't aware that anyone in my family had ever accomplished anything except being laborers and shoemakers. Then I found that one of my great-great grandfathers was a doctor and his brother had served in the Civil War and died at Andersonville Prison in Georgia. All of a sudden, I developed an interest in the Civil War.

No matter where you live, there is some historical significance to your local area. Use mental pictures to visualize historical characters as living today. Watch the History Channel, TLC and the Discovery Channel. Watch historical movies. Visit historical sites when ever possible, and study about the site before visiting it. Check your family history. Have any of your ancestors been involved in any historical incidents? When and where did they live? Where did they come from? If you could live in any time period, what would it be? Study and become an expert on that time period.

Sensory Learning Tip

Tactile Learners: If possible visit the historical sites that you are interested in and actually touch the buildings and stand on the ground where the events happened. There is something special about visiting Lexington, Concord, Appomattox and the Alamo.

✦ TIP #63
Use techniques that work best for foreign languages.

The first rule to help you in a foreign language is to choose a language you like. If you are going to be spending time learning a language, it should be one that you will find useful and one that you really want to learn.

There are also many other things you can do to help you learn another language. Find someone who speaks the language and practice on that person. If people know that you want to learn their native language, most will be glad to help you. This could also give you a personal tutor. Get a pen pal in a country where your target language is spoken and write back and forth, either with snail mail or e-mail. You could also subscribe to foreign language magazines or newspapers.

In foreign language teaching, instructors sometimes use the total immersion technique. (No, not under water.) The object is to place the student in an actual or simulated situation where everyone speaks the target language and you can feel that you are in that culture. You can simulate the same thing by putting nametags on objects. Try going through the day using only your target language. Learn all you can about the language, people and culture whose language you wish to learn. Sometimes it helps to study foreign languages with a friend or study group.

Get out those index cards to use as flash cards.

Sensory Learning Tips

Visual Learners: Use nametags or pictures of the objects that won't fit into your room.

Auditory Learners: Say the words out loud as you think about them. Listen to music in your target language. Listen to foreign language tapes or CD's.

Tactile Learners: Touch the objects as you say the name in your target language.

✦ TIP #64
Make math and science a bit easier.

You learn math and science in steps, each one building on the preceding step. So you should take it step by step, slowly if necessary to let the information sink in and gel. Make sure you understand where you are before going on. Here, too, like languages, sometimes in math and science, it may help to study with a friend.

Keep in mind that there are only 10-12 key principles in most math courses, so stick with it. Look for where your math and science could be applied in your everyday life.

Look for little tricks and shortcuts. For instance, to convert Celsius temperature to Fahrenheit temperature, add 15 to the Celsius and then double it. So, take 5 degrees Celsius, add 15 to get 20 and then double it to 40 degrees Fahrenheit. It's not 100% accurate, but it will put you in the ballpark.

Also, just as it's important to have legible handwriting in essays, make sure you print your numbers clearly and have them aligned neatly in columns. You would be surprised how many mistakes result from sloppy figures and figures not aligned clearly.

Sensory Learning Tips

Visual Learners: Keep charts and graphs, even scientific principles written on posters where you can see them often. In high school I wasn't very interested in science, but I can still remember much of the periodic chart of the elements that was on the wall of my science lab. I had to look at it every day.

Auditory Learners: Music is based on mathematics. Check it out.

Tactile Learners: Make as many charts, graphs and visuals as you can and put them on the wall. Also, do as many experiments as you can. Touch. Do.

CHAPTER 6

TIPS ON TAKING NOTES FROM LECTURES AND ORAL MATERIAL.

Even though you are being homeschooled, there will be occasions when you will need to take notes from what someone is saying, perhaps on field trips or sometimes from actual lectures. Taking notes from oral presentations requires not only unique listening skills, but also developing the ability to take accurate and reliable notes. Here are some tips.

✦ TIP #65
Develop and use a standard system.

If you have a standard method of note taking, you can use it for any kind of notes, oral, reading, personal observations or whatever. That way you don't have to figure out each time what you meant. Here's a good format.

Use a large spiral bound or loose leaf notebook and begin a new page for each note-taking session. Date each session at the top of the page, along with the name, speaker or occasion of the talk. Leave a wide right-hand margin, maybe one quarter of the page. Put your lecture notes in the left 3/4's and your comments or questions in the right-hand 1/4. Leave some space between items on the page that you can fill in later. It's also a good idea to keep your reading notes and lecture notes separate.

✦ TIP #66
Try to recognize the speaker's format.

Listen carefully to the speaker to determine what kind of organization is used in the presentation. If the speaker uses an outline, try to visualize it. Watch for foreshadowing, a hint of what the speaker is about to cover. Sometimes from the drift of the talk, you can tell that the speaker is about to make a point or give important material. If it's repeated, write it down. Repetition is a way to emphasize.

✦ TIP #67
Think before your write.

Be an active listener and try not to write down everything the speaker says. Write down only the main points or as much as you can of what you consider important. Remember, the purpose of note taking is to condense and organize. These are notes, not dictation.

✦ TIP #68
Write legibly!

Keep your notes neat and organized. You are the one who needs to re-read this stuff! It wasn't until I was in college that I learned how to take lecture notes. I discovered this when I tried to re-read my class notes during my freshman year. My handwriting was so atrocious that it was nearly impossible to read, so I had to make a very special effort to write clearly or even print.

✦ TIP #69
Don't argue–at first.

If you are listening to a presentation and the speaker says something that you disagree with, give it a little time to sink in. After the presentation and after thinking it through, if you still disagree, then you may want to address that point with the speaker. Don't disrupt the presentation with your objections. That's simply rude and in poor taste.

✦ TIP #70
Use abbreviations that you will understand later.

Abbreviations will help you save time and space in your notebook. However, right along with writing legibly is the need to use standard abbreviations that you will always recognize and that always mean the same thing every time. You may make up your own abbreviations, of course, because you are the one who will be using your notes, but using standard ones means that you won't have to make up all new ones. Here are some that may help you.

cf...........	compare (confer)
ie...........	that is
eg..........	for example
w/.........	with
w/o.......	without
&, +......	and
=..........	equals
ca.........	about (in time)
re.........	in reference to
(?)........	Something you don't understand
ck.........	Check on this.

✦ TIP #71
Review your notes immediately.

If at all possible, read over your notes as soon as you can and while the speaker is still present. If there is anything you don't understand, ask.

Sensory Learning Tips

Auditory Learners: Here, of course, is where you should do really well because you learn better by hearing the material.

Tactile Learners: Write it down.

CHAPTER 7

GETTING THE MOST FROM TEXTS

TIPS ON TAKING NOTES FROM TEXTBOOKS

Your academic achievement corresponds directly to the number and the accuracy of the notes you take. Textbooks are one of the main sources of material that you will be using, and efficient, effective note-taking from textbooks can be invaluable. Taking notes from your text also forces you to become an active reader. It is very difficult to remember everything that you read (or even half of it), but just the very fact that you write something down will help fix it in your memory.

I once had a professor, Dr. Hoover, who could lecture for hours on end on virtually any topic in history. When we asked him how he could do this without notes, he told us that when he read the original material, he re-read it and re-read it and re-read it until he know it by heart and it had become ingrained in his mind. He was a neat guy, but we did think him a bit odd. He was middle aged, refused to drive a car, lived in a one-room apartment and used an ironing board for a table. We had more important and interesting things to do than spend all of our time reading history books, over and over and over. And so do you. Good note taking should help you avoid having to do this.

There is an acronym that should apply to many human endeavors. It is the KISS principle. Keep It Simple, Student. The reason for this is that many people have the tendency to make things complicated and then mess that up. What you want to do is take complete and accurate notes but keep the process as simple as possible.

What about highlighting? If you own the book, of course you may write in the margin and underline relevant parts. But even these two options have some drawbacks. Most people who underline or highlight, underline or highlight too much. And even writing notes in the margin of the text is more passive than writing more complete notes in a notebook. Besides that, what are you going to underline? Just what's important? Everything in the book should be important. Just the topic sentences? Then you could just go back and re-read them without underlining. If you insist on underlining or highlighting, do it sparingly, probably no more than 10% of the material in the text. And even at that, it's no substitute for note taking.

Taking speaking and reading notes in the same format is a good idea. Here are some tips to help you take effective reading notes.

✦ TIP #72
Use the same system as for lecture notes.

Use a large spiral bound or loose leaf notebook for each subject or one with clear divisions for each subject. Begin a new page for each note taking session. Date each session at the top of the page, along with the name of the book and chapter or page numbers. Set up your notebook page the same way. Leave a wide right-hand margin for your own observations, comments and questions.

✦ TIP #73
Get a general idea of the reading.

You can get the general drift of the reading by looking over the introduction, pictures, captions, table of contents, even the index. After you have a pretty good indication of what the stuff is all about, then go back and read your assignment carefully.

✦ TIP #74
Now, actually taking the notes.

Summarize. Remember, don't copy directly from the book or take notes on everything. If you use the book's exact words, a direct quotation, use quotation marks, like this"–". If you para-phrase the text, using you own words, you don't need quotation marks. Try not to just copy titles and sub-titles. This becomes mechanical and prevents your actually thinking about what you are taking notes on. Summarize each paragraph if necessary. Sometimes you can summarize by topics. Outline the text if that helps. (My tenth grade biology teacher had us outline the whole book, one chapter at a time.) It will give you a good overview and good framework to which to add subsequent material. Remember, write legibly! You will have to read this later.

✦ TIP #75
Make friends with the photocopier.

Sometimes when you have a lot of material in lists or in con-centrated form, try photocopying the page so you can take that with you to study. There's no point wasting your time copying down in detail what you can much more easily photocopy.

✦ TIP #76
What to do after you are finished.

Read over your notes as soon as you are done with the reading assignment. It will help establish the material in your long-term memory. And before beginning the next reading assignment, re-read the notes you took on the last assignment. Repetition!!!

✦ TIP #77
Try a visual outlining technique

There is another way to take notes from texts and lectures. This technique is variously called Mapping, Concept Mapping, Networking, Graphic Overview, Clustering, Visual Outlining and Webbing. Regardless of what it is called, the concept is basically the same. It can be used for a variety of purposes, but is probably best for review and seeing the overall concept being studied. It can be a very effective way to organize and concentrate large amounts of material because one page of mapping could illustrate 10-20 pages of text.

Here is the general idea behind mapping. Use a blank sheet of paper. In the center of that paper write the topic and circle it. Now, as you read, or review, draw lines out from the central topic and jot down other notes and ideas relating to it, making an idea chain. The object is to get the material down on paper to get the overall concept. Don't worry too much about the arrangement of the notes or the logic you may be following–or lack of it. An idea chain may branch many times as you write down your notes.

If ideas have a common theme, draw a large circle around them. To show relationships between ideas, draw arrows between them. You can improvise other shortcuts and abbreviations of your own.

Some students also use this method of taking notes from texts and oral presentations, but it is probably best used to review material already covered. However, remember that however the technique works for you, use it.

Once you have finished reading a text, close the book and use the mapping technique to review what you have read. Write down the central idea and then everything you can remember about the text. When you have finished with the map, open the book and review what you may have missed. Now write that down too.

Sensory Learning Tips

Visual Learners: This technique lets you see graphically the material illustrated on the page.

Auditory Learners: Say it out loud as you do it.

Tactile Learners: Just writing down the material will help you to remember it. Trace the lines with your finger as you review.

✦ TIP #78
Another way you can get through reading material faster and understand more–PRQR.

Reading efficiently is a valuable skill that can save you time. Because we read different material for different purposes, we read in different ways and at different speeds. The way we read novels, short stories and magazine articles is probably not the best way to read textbooks. The former we read for entertainment, but textbooks are for the transfer of information from the writer to the reader and should be not only read, but also studied. So, we should have an efficient method to get through the material as quickly as possible (but probably not as quickly as a novel or short story) and still learn from it.

Several reading/study techniques have been developed to help the reader get more from textbooks. The bases of all of these techniques are similar and have been debated by reading specialists for many years. The important thing is that you have a system that works for you.

The PRQR method is simple and easy to use and will help you become an active, involved reader. It stands for PREVIEW, READ, QUESTION, and REVIEW.

Try using the PRQR method for all reading assignments, especially the ones you consider dull and subjects you are having trouble with. It's simple and some parts of it you probably do already. It is especially good because it provides two and three times exposure to the material.

PREVIEW THE MATERIAL

This is pre-reading. It is looking over the reading material without really reading the text. When you pick up a magazine, do you start reading the text right away? I'll bet not. If you are like me, you start with the pictures and titles and maybe the captions under the pictures. Check textual and non-textual material. Skim the text quickly to get an over-all picture of the subject. Try reading topic sentences. Check the title page. This will allow you to check the date to be sure the information is current. Check introduction and preface, index, table of contents as well. Make sure the author has credibility in the field he is writing about.

Check introductory paragraphs, headings and topic sentences. This preview should give you an idea of what concepts and ideas are discussed. It should give you such a good overview that it's almost like cheating–except this is honest.

READ

Next, actually read the text. It should be easier now because you already have an idea of what it is about. You have already looked at the pictures! After each paragraph, pause and say out loud what you have read, then after each page. Remember, hearing yourself say it will improve you chances of retaining the information. Do your reading with pen in hand to take text notes. Again, just the act of writing it down will help you remember.

QUESTION

Now, after you have finished reading and taking notes, jot down some questions about the text that you would ask in a quiz on the material. Use the 5 W's and H (Who, What, Where, When, Why and How). Write them down and then write answers for them. You may have to look back over the text for information.

REVIEW

After jotting down the questions, review the material once more using the notes you have taken. Do it out loud.

The PRQR technique will take a little more time than simply reading the text, but should be well worth it.

SENSORY LEARNING TIPS

Auditory Learners: Talk to yourself as you read. Ask questions and review out loud.

Tactile Learners: Skim your finger along as you read the text. Touch the pictures.

✦ TIP #79
Learn how to increase your reading speed in 15 minutes

This is not a book on speed reading or even reading skills, but there is one simple technique that I have used with students to help them increase their reading speed and improve retention.

This is a beginning technique that is used in some speed-reading courses. Actually, you could get your reading speed as fast as 1000 words per minute, but it is difficult to get over that speed with only this technique. However, if you are reading at the average speed of about 250 words per minute, and you double that to 500 words per minute, you will have to spend only half as much time reading assignments. (Or you could read twice as much in the same time.)

It is very simple. First, choose a passage for reading. With someone to time you, read the passage as you normally would. If you're by yourself, use a kitchen timer. When you reach five minutes, have that person stop you. Count the number of words in the passage and divide by five. That is your reading speed in words per minute.

Next, choose a similar passage from the same book. This time, move your index finger to run along just under the words, serving as a guide for where your eyes should be. Keep your finger moving at a steady pace, one that your eyes can easily follow. Gradually increase the movement of your finger to the point where your eyes can just keep up with the speed and still read the words.

What this does is force your eyes to move at a steady, and hopefully faster, speed and will help prevent you from moving your eyes back to re-read previous material. With a little practice, this will definitely help to speed up your reading.

Even when you get good at this technique, keep in mind we read different material at different speeds. You cannot read the directions for setting the time on your digital watch at the same speed that you can read a magazine article.

Sensory Learning Tip

Tactile Learners: Here, touching the material is really necessary and will help you to learn this technique.

✦ TIP #80
Read out loud.

Sometimes, especially if you feel that you have trouble reading, try reading out loud. You can read to other people or just to yourself. I don't mean out loud as in moving your lips with no sound coming out. I mean out loud out loud—in a speaking voice. You would be surprised how much this will help you remember and help you with your reading.

Sensory Learning Tip

Auditory Learners: It may be actually hearing your own voice that helps you learn this way.

✦ TIP #81
Too tired to read? Here's a quick fix.

Have you ever been reading and just felt too tired, but it's material you have to get through? Try standing up to read. It will help you stay awake and alert. You might also try pacing the floor while you are reading–just watch where you are going.

This is not to say that you should study when you are really tired. This technique should be used when you just feel a bit drowsy, like we all do sometimes, maybe on a warm afternoon. If it is late at night and you are beat, go to bed and get some rest.

✦ TIP #82
Find answers quickly.

Sometimes, when we are confronted with an assignment that requires finding answers by doing some research, we aren't always sure just where to start. Whether it is for your school work or just for your own curiosity, what you are actually looking for is called data. Data is any kind of information, including whatever answers you may need.

Let's start with books. If there is an index, check it for key words. Check the table of contents and look over what each chapter is about. Depending on how the book is organized, check the topic headings. Check topic sentences in paragraphs.

Don't forget the old standbys, dictionaries and encyclopedias. They are still reliable references. Just make sure they are current, especially the encyclopedias. You don't want to look for answers to scientific or technical questions in an encyclopedia that was printed in 1970. Dictionaries change more slowly, but they do change with the language, as words change meaning, are lost or more often, added to the language.

In addition to the books you are using, the Internet is a powerful tool for research. Type your search topic into Google or another search engine and see what results it returns. But don't stop with Google. There are hundreds of Internet search engines available for your use, and each will return slightly different results. Some of them even combine the results of other search engines. Here are some of the most useful:

About.com	\<http:home.about.com>
Alta Vista	\<http:www.altavista.com>
AOL Anywhere	\<http:search.aol.com>
Ask.com	\<http.www.ask.com>
Dogpile	\<http:www.dogpile.com>
Excite	\<http:www.excite.com>
Go.com	\<http:www.go.com>
Hotbot	\<http:www.hotbot.com>
Lycos	\<http:www.lycos.com>
Metacrawler	\<http:www.metacrawler.com>
MSN	\<http.search.msn.com>
Webcrawler	\<http:www.webcrawler.com>
Yahoo	\<http:www.yahoo.com>

Caution: Be aware that sometimes even an innocent search request could return some salacious web sites. (That means dirty, sexually explicit.) Sometimes, even with filters in place, this could happen. If it does, clicking the back button will probably not get you free of the site. You must click the down arrow in the address window and scroll down to another web site. Also, explain to your parents what happened. Remember, there is a record of all web sites visited, and it is better coming from you than having them find out some other way.

CHAPTER 8

WRITING TIPS

You can't avoid it. You must learn to write well. That is, well enough to make yourself understood. Keep in mind the three goals of good writing:

1. Say exactly what you have to say.
2. Say it in as few words as possible.
3. Say it so that it cannot be misunderstood.

Some students have trouble organizing their ideas when writing. Indeed, sometimes they know what they want to write about, but after that, they don't quite know how or where to start. There are some techniques that you can use to help you develop your ideas into an essay or report.

✦ TIP #83
Understand the process of writing.

One of the most helpful ways to learn to improve your writing is to understand the writing process. This involves understanding a model for writing and concentrating a little more on the actual process of writing in order to improve the final product–your paper. The process can be broken down into as many as eight steps, but it is easiest to explain using only five.

PLANNING

This is everything you do before you actually start to write your paper. It is what you think about, what you discuss, what notes you jot down and any research you do. It is considering the points that you want to express and who you are writing for, your audience. This is also where you decide how you want to organize your paper.

WRITING (DRAFTING)

This is when the pencil meets the paper–or the fingers hit the keys. It is also called drafting, like first draft, second draft, and so on. This is when you actually begin to write the paper.

REVISING, RE-WRITING

This is the stage when you re-read your work out loud, and maybe have someone else read it for you so you can share ideas about it and evaluate what you have written so far. This is also when you make revisions to your paper, and it is probably where you will spend the most time and effort. Revising is at least 60% of writing well.

EDITING, PROOFREADING

This is when you fix the proofreading errors, the typos and the misspellings, correct any punctuation errors and smooth out the sentences. You are preparing your final copy, or draft. This is the stage where you fix *the* for the word you wanted to say, *they*.

SUBMITTING, PUBLISHING

This is the point at which you make your paper known to the world, making it public, which is what publishing means. At least, this is when you turn it in to your teacher.

Now you know the model; let's look at it more realistically. I don't know anyone who writes in such a precise, logical manner. I certainly don't. I may start planning with a brief outline or a couple of random notes, but then I may start the actual writing also. And then I may go back to gather some additional material. Or when I am writing, I may get a great idea to use later. You see, writing is an organic process—it grows. It is flexible and moldable. People jump back and forth when they write, which means that your technique for writing is probably different from another person's technique. But still, having a good model can help to explain the writing process.

OK. Now that you have that background, here are some ways to help you develop your ideas for writing. Most of this involves the foundation of your paper, the planning or organizing stage. That's where you start and where the foundation for your paper is laid, both in content and form.

Let's say you know what you want to write about, but where do you go now? Try these ways to help you develop your idea, your thesis.

✦ TIP #84
Brainstorming

This technique works best with a group of people, but you can do it by yourself also. You simply jot down as many ideas about your topic as you can think of in a set period of time, say five or ten minutes. Write down any idea that comes to mind, no matter how ridiculous it may be. Make no judgment about it until you are finished. When you are done, look over the list and use those ideas that seem most plausible.

✦ TIP #85
Five W's

This one should actually be called Five W's and an H. It stands for Who, What, Where, When, Why–and How. This is a technique that is taught in journalism classes to get all the facts. Just as you would do if you were a newspaper reporter, you write down these words and then after each, answer that question. Who is involved? What happened? Where did it happen? When did it happen? Why did it happen? And how did it happen?

✦ TIP #86
Alphabet Cueing

We mentioned Alphabet Cueing earlier in our discussion on memory, but it can also be helpful in developing your writing ideas. List the alphabet along the left side of a sheet of paper. Then after each letter, write whatever that letter suggests about your topic. For some letters, you may have nothing. For others, you may have several ideas.

✦ TIP #87
Five Senses Cueing

This is especially useful if you are writing a description. List the five senses—sight, sound, touch, taste and smell. Then, after each word, write what that sense would suggest about the topic.

For example, what would your individual senses detect if you were walking along a country road in a snowstorm? What you see is pretty obvious. Sight is where we get perhaps 90% of the input to our brain. What do you hear? The snow crunching beneath your feet? If it's very quiet in a snowstorm, sometimes you can actually hear the snow falling. What do you feel? Cold, right? How about the snow hitting your face? What do you smell? How about wood smoke from a fireplace? Taste? Come on, you stick your tongue out and catch some snowflakes.

✦ TIP #88:
Webbing

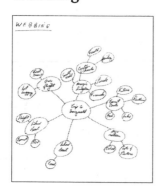

You can use Webbing to develop ideas for a composition just as you do for taking notes from your reading or for review. Begin by writing the topic in the center of a piece of paper and circling it. Then draw lines out from your main topic to whatever other ideas on the topic you have. As one idea leads to another, draw a line from the old idea to the new one. If you have a completely different thought, begin a new chain leading out from the main topic. Some chains may be short, one or two circles, and some may be long and branch several times. It is a sort of graphic outlining.

✦ TIP #89
Free Writing

In Free Writing, you take a blank piece of paper, a pen or pencil and begin writing about the topic. The rules are that you must continue writing for a specified period of time, maybe five or ten minutes. You may not stop until that time is up. You may write anything about the topic. This is one time when spelling and grammar don't count. The only important thing is to get ideas down on paper. When the time is up, then evaluate what you have written–for ideas only. There will probably be some junk that you don't want to use, but there should be some good stuff too.

✦ TIP #90
Outlining

Outlining is still useful for developing ideas for writing, and it is probably the one technique that most people are familiar with. Your outline doesn't have to be formal or balanced. That is, it doesn't have to have a B for every A or a 2 for every 1. Make it a simple outline that you can follow easily, and that you can add to as you go along. It's OK to scribble notes or add items in the margin. In the same way that a dump truck is not used for show, but for work, this is a working outline. It's all right to have it look a bit messy.

✦ TIP #91
Self Interviewing

In Self Interviewing, you write down a bunch of questions about your topic as if you knew absolutely nothing about it. Try to make your mind totally blank about your topic. Then you answer those questions. You might want to start with the Five W's and go on from there. When you finish answering the questions, you should have a good basis for the essay.

CHAPTER 9

SHARPEN YOUR LISTENING AND SPEAKING SKILLS

LISTENING SKILLS TIPS

Home school systems vary greatly in structure, from the rigid and tightly scheduled to the more informal to the really relaxed format. But the principles of learning are universal. Just because you sit in a "class" listening to what is going on around you, doesn't mean you are either studying or learning. To get the most out of your education, you will have to learn to become an active listener.

One of the most overlooked skills is the skill of listening, and let's understand right from the start that hearing is not listening. We hear lots of sounds everyday in background noise, but we don't really listen to most of it. In fact, we filter out most background noise. You will have many occasions to learn from listening, both in your school and out of school. Perhaps it is your parent teaching you in a lecture format or a "guest" speaker who will be talking. Active listening means that you are making a conscious effort not only to hear what the person is saying, but also to digest, understand and perhaps respond to it.

Here are some tips that will help you become an active listener.

✦ TIP #92
Give the speaker your full attention.

Look at the speaker. Make eye contact. Have you ever tried to carry on a conversation with a person who has the TV on in the background? Invariably, his eyes wander to the TV set. We break eye contact naturally sometimes, just so the speaker doesn't think we are weird. But don't look out of the window or at other things going on in the room. Constantly looking someplace other than at the speaker is simply rude. To indicate your interest, you may want to use your body language and lean slightly toward the speaker.

✦ TIP #93
Give feedback to the speaker.

It is very disconcerting to a speaker to talk to an audience that just sits there looking like envelopes with no addresses on them. Just imagine talking to one of your friends and not receiving a nod, smile, or even a frown. One of the most basic methods of communication is body language (Perhaps it is the most basic). Likewise, when you are listening to a speaker, nod once in a while. Maybe smile occasionally to let the speaker know that you are still awake.

✦ TIP # 94
Consciously focus on what the speaker is saying.

In addition to giving the speaker feedback, try to really concentrate on what he is saying. Don't let other sounds interfere with hearing the ideas the speaker is attempting to convey to you. We can normally think about four times faster than we can speak, so try not to let your mind wander. If you do find your mind wandering, change your position in the seat and refocus.

✦ TIP #95
Take notes carefully.

If you are taking notes, write down only the main points. You can fill in details later, and you may want to formulate questions that you may want to ask the speaker later.

✦ TIP #96
When you want to speak, wait until the speaker has finished.

There are few things that are more irritating to a speaker than to be cut off in the middle of a sentence by someone butting in. How do you feel when someone interrupts when you are trying to make a point? It is just common courtesy to wait your turn, even in private conversations.

✦ TIP #97
Don't jump to judgment.

Do not judge what the speaker has said until after you have heard him out and had a chance to digest the ideas. First, hear what the speaker is saying. Then understand what the speaker is saying. And then evaluate and respond to what the speaker is saying.

SPEAKING SKILLS TIPS

Most people have no problem speaking. It is speaking in front of a group that bothers them. Speaking in front of a group is the most common fear that people have, even more than the fear of spiders, snakes or death. It puts us into an unfamiliar situation, one where we feel uncomfortable. The irony of this is that it is the least grounded fear of all. What we really fear is making a fool of ourselves, not looking good and possibly, subconsciously, being rejected.

Like all skills, speaking to a group gets easier with practice. The more you do it, the more comfortable you should be with it and the better you should be able to speak in front of other people. It's a paradox, really. In order to get good at what you fear, you have to do the thing you fear. Here are some tips to help you with your public speaking.

✦ TIP #98
Fear not.

Fear not, for they shall not harm you. Usually, your audience will be rooting for you. They don't want to be up there talking either, so they will be kind. (Unless you see that each of them is holding a stone suitable for throwing, you are safe. Fear your audience only if each of them does have a rock—then run.)

✦ TIP #99
What is there to lose?

What's really at stake here? No one is going to attack you. No one is going to threaten you. Chances are very good that you will finish without any bruises whatsoever. Remember that unless you are a brain surgeon, most of what we do in any kind of school is practice. (Come to think of it, brain surgeons call it a practice, too.)

✦ TIP #100
Prepare...Prepare...Prepare.

This point cannot be stressed too much. Some people have the gift of gab–they talk a lot and easily. Most people don't. But even those people who speak easily in front of a group, tend to wander from the topic. If you are one of those who is gabby, you need to prepare to make sure you cover what you want to cover. That means preparing carefully. If you are someone who doesn't speak easily in front of a group, preparing will help you stay on track and give you some confidence in what you are saying. Preparing isn't just practicing, although that is part of it. Preparing means gathering all the material you will need, researching your topic, organizing your material and notes, and being in control of all your resources. Before you get up to talk, make sure you have your presentation well prepared and well rehearsed.

✦ TIP #101
Don't be afraid to use notes.

There is nothing wrong with using notes. Many professional speakers still use notes. I used to keep them taped to the back of the presentation board when I would conduct seminars. I didn't refer to them, but it was nice to know they were there. The best kind of notes to use are those that will fit onto index cards, the 3x5 inch kind. Unless you need statistics, which may be better presented in a graphic, all you should need is a couple of words on each card to remind you of where you are in the talk and to make sure you cover all the points that you plan to cover. The less conspicuous the notes, the better. If you really need an outline, use one sheet and lay it down in an inconspicuous place (on the lectern is fine) when you get up to speak. Avoid using a bunch of papers that you have to shuffle and maybe get out of order. And don't try to memorize your talk. Chances are that you may go blank in the middle of your presentation.

✦ TIP #102
Practice…Practice…Practice.

Be sure to practice what you are presenting at least 3-5 times out loud in front of a mirror or another person. Again, do not try to memorize what you want to say. If you practice out loud five times and use a few note cards as reminders, you should have internalized the essence of what you want to say and what specific points you want to get across to your audience.

✦ TIP #103
Go there.

We are more comfortable in familiar settings, so if you will be giving the talk in an unfamiliar place, visit the site before you have to do the talk. Stand where you will be standing for the talk. Look around the room and get used to it. That way, you will be familiar with the room and should be more relaxed when you have to talk there.

✦ TIP #104
Speak up.

Speak loudly enough so that the last person in the last row can hear you. In the long run, even if you have prepared the best speech the world has ever heard, the world may never hear it if you don't speak up. Your speech can't be good until it is loud enough to be heard.

✦ TIP #105
Look 'em in the eye.

Maintain eye contact. Look at the people and move your eyes around the room every few minutes. Eye contact draws in your audience and makes them part of the presentation. If someone intimidates you, don't look at that person. Pick out three people in different parts of the room who look friendly and talk to them. This will help you maintain eye contact with the audience as a whole.

✦ TIP #106
Look up when you are reading.

If you are reading a selection, look up once in a while. Use your finger or a 3x5 card to help keep track of where you are on the page. Then when you look at the audience, your eyes should always come back to the right location. With practice, you can maintain eye contact with your audience about 30-50% of the time you are reading.

✦ TIP #107
Use visuals and props.

Any kind of audio-visual aid will help your presentation. This could be a power-point presentation from your laptop (if you are fortunate enough to have one), or just a simple list displayed on an easel of what you want to talk about, which is also a clever way to build in your notes. It could be a handout, a poster on the wall or an object you can show or pass around your audience. A bonus here is that using visuals will direct your listeners' attention to that visual and not so much at you. That should help your self-confidence.

✦ TIP #108
When you're done, you're not quite done.

It's a good idea at the end of your talk to give your audience a brief review of what you have covered, stressing the main points. Then, return to your seat (unless, of course, you are taking questions from the audience). But wait! When you finish, don't just quickly dash back to your seat. We know that you just want to be done. However, don't make it too obvious because that just makes you look silly after a good talk. So, pause for a second, smile sincerely, as if giving an unspoken thank you, and then take your seat. You will look so much more mature–and elegant, suave and sophisticated–that way.

SENSORY LEARNING TIPS

Visual Learners: When you have to give a talk, make use of visuals as much as possible. It will help you, and remember that even your audience is composed primarily of visual learners.

Auditory Learners: After you have practiced your talk, try recording and listening to it.

Tactile Learners: It's especially good for you to use visuals and props, things that you can handle, and it adds interest to your talk.

CHAPTER 10

TEST TAKING TECHNIQUES

Even though you are homeschooled, you can't avoid having your educational progress evaluated from time to time. Someone has to figure out just how much you know about various subjects. Most of the time, that evaluation will take the form of tests. It is the only practical way that you can be certain that you have actually learned the material and just how well you have mastered it. However, you can be smart in knowing how to handle different types of tests.

✦ TIP # 109
Understand different types of tests and how best to approach them.

The tests you will be taking are two types, objective and subjective. Objective tests attempt to measure pretty much factual information. They are short-answer, matching, multiple choice, true-false, and fill-in-the-blank. Subjective tests involve factual information presented in an essay format. They test not only your recall of factual data, but also your ability to relate that data in a structured, written format. They could involve using logic to prove your case or opinion.

Before we look at the specifics of taking either type of test, here are some general tips on taking any kind of test.

✦ TIP #110
Make sure you have gotten a good night's sleep and are not hungry.

There is just no substitute for rest. You need to be refreshed to be at your best during test time, so make sure you have gotten your eight hours or whatever you need to be sharp when the test paper is handed to you.

Also, have something light to eat before the test. Don't have too much to eat or the blood goes to your stomach instead of your brain. Avoid sugar and too many carbohydrates. The first revs your engine and the second slows you down.

✦ TIP #111
Look over the test before you begin answering questions.

When you get the test, look over it briefly to see how long it is. Read all the directions carefully! Let me say that again: Read all the directions carefully! Did I make my point?

Look quickly over the questions. All this should give you an idea of how much time will be involved in completing the test. Check this against how much time you have available. Now, plan your time. Allow some time at the end to review and in case an emergency arises.

HOW TO PREPARE FOR OBJECTIVE TESTS

Now, let's look first at the best techniques to get ready for objective tests. These tests check your instant recall of specific information. They are designed to challenge your reasoning and independent thinking. They don't always present obvious answers, and sometimes you have to make fine distinctions between two or more possible answers.

How do you know if you are ready for the test and what you should be looking for? Well, can you recall specific terms, facts, names and other key words? Do you know the vocabulary and terms pertaining to the subject? Can you distinguish ways in which ideas, facts, theories and other material are similar or different?

✦ TIP #112
Review your text and notes.

This should be a snap if you have been reviewing all along. Get all of your notes that are relevant for the test in front of you. Systematically review all of them and look over the text.

✦ TIP #113
See if you can list the major concepts.

Without referring to your text or notes, try to list the major concepts that you covered in your classes. You might want to try the mapping technique here to help you recall and organize your ideas.

✦ TIP #114
Review the vocabulary of the subject.

Every subject has its own unique vocabulary. For instance, the word *desensitization* would belong to psychology and *genus* to botany. Again, use 3x5 flash cards to help you study and review.

✦ TIP #115
Review out loud.

All types of learners can benefit from this, but auditory learners could find this especially helpful. As you are reviewing, verbalize your answers. Hearing them will help to reinforce the data in your long-term memory.

Sensory Learning Tip

Auditory Learners: It helps not only to review out loud, but you might also try having another person ask you some practice questions verbally.

✦ TIP #116
When applicable, make visual aids.

Construct charts, tables, lists and diagrams of the subject material. This is in addition to what you made when you were studying the subject. Re-do them from memory. Compare and contrast when you can. Form associations with and within the material.

Sensory Learning Tip

Tactile Learners: Tactile learners take note!

✦ TIP #117
Write it down as you review.

Remember? Just the act of writing it down will help to reinforce the material in your long-term memory. Write it down as you review.

HOW TO TAKE OBJECTIVE TESTS

✦ TIP #118
Jot down any notes that you want to recall.

After you receive the test, and you have had a chance to look over the format, make some brief notes on material that you want to keep in mind. Make sure the person giving the test is aware that you are writing them down and that he or she knows they are not crib sheets or prepared "student reference cards."

✦ TIP #119
Read the directions again.

Re-read the directions very carefully for each section to be sure you understand them. Do not skip the directions! They may ask you to print and use block letters or answer 3 out of 4 of the questions instead of all of them.

✦ TIP #120
Answer the easiest questions first.

Always answer the easiest questions first and begin with the section of the test that will yield the most points. Save the harder questions for later. The reason for this is simple. Harder questions will involve more concentration and sometimes the process of elimination to determine the correct answer. Easier questions do not require as much time for these processes. Answering the easier questions first will help avoid getting caught short on time later.

✦ TIP #121
Do not let any answer blank.

If it is blank, it is wrong. If you have to guess, you at least have a chance that it is right. (Let's not call it guessing. Let's call it the educated elimination technique!) Do your guessing after you have answered all the questions you know.

✦ TIP #122
Note key words in each question.

As you read the questions, be careful to note words that indicate the nature of the question. Some key words to watch for are *How*, *What*, *Why*, *Who*, *When* and *Where*. For instance, if the test asks *what* were the causes of the American Civil War, your response should be different from your answer to the question of *why* the South seceded from the Union.

✦ TIP #123
Don't try to second-guess the question.

Read the question literally. If there is ambiguity in the answers, choose the most logical one and write a note about the ambiguity on the test. Most teachers will respect your observation and, if your point is valid, give you credit for the answer.

✦ TIP #124
Sometimes, reverse may be a good gear.

If you are going through an objective-question test where you are answering a lot of the same type questions in quick succession, you may feel overwhelmed or fatigued. Try reversing direction, going to the end of that section and working backward. It may help to keep your mind on its toes–so to speak.

MULTIPLE CHOICE QUESTIONS

✦ TIP #125
Eliminate obviously wrong answers.

As you read the questions and the possible answers, try drawing a line through the ones that are obviously wrong. Often this technique can get you down to two possible answers.

✦ TIP #126
Read the question as if it had no answer.

Another thing that you may want to try is to answer the question by filling in an answer before you even look at the options. Then check possible answers against yours.

✦ TIP #127
Read the question separately each time with each answer.

Try reading the question with the first possible answer, then the second and third, and so on. Try saying it to yourself in a one-foot voice (That's a whisper that cannot be heard beyond one foot). You may also want to try reading it as if it were a true or false question.

✦ TIP #128
Be careful when you see words like *not, but* and *except*.

The words *not, but* and *except* can very subtly trick the reader because they will limit the answer. Be careful with them.

✦ TIP #129
Also, be careful when the question contains absolute words.

Words like *always, never* and *only* are called absolutes and are deal-killers. They mean "without exception." Be on the lookout for these words in multiple-choice questions. Answers containing absolute words are usually incorrect.

✦ TIP #130
Select the option that gives the most complete and accurate information.

Short answers are more likely to be incorrect because they are simplistic and may contain absolute words. In general, the longer and more complete the answer, the more likely it is to be correct.

✦ TIP #131
If you are offered "all of the above"...

Sometimes, try as you may, you just can't come up with the correct answer. They all look good. In this case, if you are offered "All of the above," take it. It is most likely the correct answer.

✦ TIP #132
Make educated guesses and eliminate answers any way you can.

Use your native intelligence and what you have learned from your studies to make what is called an educated guess. This is not just guessing. It is guessing, based on your knowledge, through the process of elimination. The more answers you can eliminate, the better your chances are for choosing the correct answer. If you have four answers to choose from, you have a one in four chance of being right. If you can eliminate two possible answers to have two remaining possibilities and you have to guess, you have even money on getting the right answer—that's 50% instead of 25%. The odds are better.

TRUE-FALSE QUESTIONS

✦ TIP #133
If you have to guess, your odds are 50-50 on true-false questions.

You have a percentage advantage with true-false questions if you really must guess. Your chances of being right are 50-50. But then your chances of being wrong are also 50-50. Guess only if you must. An educated guess is best, but any guess is better than leaving the answer blank. Remember, a blank answer is 100% wrong.

✦ TIP #134
For a statement to be true, it must be 100% true all of the time.

In true-false questions, if the statement is not true all of the time in all cases, the answer is false. It can't be true some of the time or even most of the time. It must be true *all* of the time.

✦ TIP #135
If any part of the statement is false, the whole thing is false.

This is the other side of the coin because just as for a true-false statement to be true, it must be true all of the time, so too if any part of the statement is false, the whole thing is false. (How would you like to fly in an airplane that lands safely *most* of the time?) It's like a weak link in an otherwise strong chain. Often in true-false questions, it could be very subtle, such as having names, dates and details mixed-up or misleading.

✦ TIP #136
Test-makers often play word games with true-false questions.

Objective questions are often word exercises where the author of the question will try to trip you up. Be cautious with words like *usually*, *some*, and *not*. They frequently mean the statement is true.

✦ TIP #137
Again, beware of word games.

We mentioned this with absolute words, but it bears repeating. Test makers often use not only absolute words, but also limiting words such as *sometimes, seldom,* and *occasionally.* Always read the question carefully and think about exactly what it is asking.

MATCHING QUESTIONS

✦ TIP #138
First, determine the ground rules.

The ground rules mean understanding the directions completely. And it doesn't hurt to ask if you are in doubt. For instance, determine if answers may be used more than once, or if there is one answer in column B for each item in column A.

✦ TIP #139
Work from one side or the other.

Don't jump back and forth. That will only waste time and confuse you. It is easier to work from the column with the most words or longest definitions. This way you won't have to read longer items when searching for a short answer.

✦ TIP #140
Cross out the ones you have used.

Keep a visual record of the answers you have used. When you have used an item in the column you are selecting from, draw a line through it. It will save time and help prevent re-reading answers you have already used.

✦ TIP #141
Look for the relationship between the columns.

Sometimes the relationship between the columns is clear, as when column B defines terms in column A. Sometimes it is not. Does an item in column A cause an item in column B? Does it precede it? Result from it? Try to find some kind of relationship.

✦ TIP #142
Here's what to do when you get your test back.

What should you do when you get your test back? Most students fail to realize that regardless of how you did on a test or quiz, analyzing the test when you get it back is also a valuable learning experience. Look over the test. What questions did you get wrong? Why did you get them wrong? Check out the correct answers. Write them on your test paper next to your incorrect answers, which you have crossed out. Did you misread the question or did you just not know the answer? Find the answer now.

Keep the test to review for any subsequent tests on the same material. Remember that what is important is how well you know the material, not how well you did on the test. But, if you know the material, you should also do well on the tests.

HOW TO PREPARE FOR SUBJECTIVE /ESSAY TESTS

Essay tests are a favorite of teachers because they test not only factual information, but also your ability to assimilate, organize and explain information and concepts that you have now placed into your long-term memory.

✦ TIP #143
Preparing for an essay test should begin long before test-time.

Preparation for essay tests should begin when you start studying the subject and continue throughout your study. Taking good notes and continuing good study habits will eliminate the necessity to cram for the test. If you understand basic concepts, theories and principles of the subject, you have a good foundation for the essay test.

✦ TIP #144
Before the test, write some sample essay questions.

Practice! A good way to practice is to write some sample questions that you think may be asked of you. Then prepare the answers for those questions and actually write them out. Make sure you know the details. (The devil is in the details.) This will help you anticipate the questions and give you on-the-ground experience.

HOW TO TAKE SUBJECTIVE/ESSAY TESTS

✦ TIP #145
Schedule your time carefully.

When you get the test in your hot little hands, look over it carefully. On an essay test, even more than on an objective test, it is easy to lose track of time and end up with too much test left and too little time. Check how many essay questions you are required to answer. It is only one? Is it three out of four? Is it all of them? Then plan your time accordingly. If you have an hour to answer three essay questions, then you should plan to devote twenty minutes to each one. Be sure to allow about ten percent of the time for preparing your answer and about ten percent for proofreading and editing.

✦ TIP #146
Read the questions very carefully.

A quick reading of the question could lead you to write an answer to the wrong question. Make sure you understand exactly what the question is asking. If you are not sure, ask your teacher. Underline key words and what you are being asked to do. Be able to distinguish between words like *detail*, *trace*, *explain*, *comment*, *prove* and *defend*. Each one is asking something different. It may help to rephrase the question in your own words, keeping the same meaning as the original question.

✦ TIP #147
Do the easiest questions first.

This works the same as with objective questions. No matter what kind of test you are taking, it is always a good idea to do the easiest questions first. The reason is simple. The easiest are the ones that should take the least amount of time to complete. If you get the easiest ones out of the way first, you will have more time to concentrate on the tough questions, which may take more time. You don't want to spend time doing the hard ones first and get caught short on time before you even get to the easier questions. Make sense?

✦ TIP #148
Organize your answer.

You could use any of several pre-writing techniques to organize, but probably the best one here is simply to outline your answer. You need not use complete sentences; remember you are working against a time limit. Just make a quick word and phrase outline, which you can add to and modify as you go along. Your outline should contain at least three supporting statements for your thesis. It should help you to organize your thoughts and also indicate to your teacher that you have thought out your answer to the question. As a rule of thumb, allow about 10% of your time to planning your answer and another 10% for proofreading and editing your answer.

Do this for each essay question before you begin writing answers for any of them. Remember to keep it flexible so that you can add ideas that pop into your head as you are writing. This will help to keep your mind from going blank toward the end of the test. Also, having the knowledge that you have already laid the groundwork for the answer may help keep you calm as you write. (It also doesn't hurt that having a brief outline really impresses teachers—even if they are your parents.)

✦ TIP #149
Write your answer carefully.

Use complete sentences—no fragments or run-ons. The first sentence of your answer should be a thesis sentence, which summarizes your answer and states your main point. Do not waste time writing an introduction, and don't use trite phrases such as *in this day and age*, *in today's world* and *now-a-days*. Make sure each paragraph has a topic sentence and thoroughly develop that idea in the paragraph.

✦ TIP #150
Penmanship counts.

Be sure your handwriting is legible! Write neatly with good penmanship and leave adequate margins. Use a pen or #2 lead pencil, something that is easy to read. Avoid erasures, but if you must erase, do it neatly. Use Whiteout if necessary. No matter who is giving the test, your parent or someone else, it is frustrating to attempt reading a messy paper with poor handwriting.

Your paper is not being compared to 30 other ones in a traditional classroom, but sloppy papers and poor handwriting are still a challenge to your reader. Sometimes—maybe—it's possible (but probably not with your parents/teachers) you may receive a lower grade just because it's hard to read your handwriting. Can you believe that?

✦ TIP # 151
Develop your paragraphs.

After your topic sentence, start providing factual information to support it. Work in as many hard facts and details as you can in the time allotted. This will help keep you from just piling on words and adding fluff to fill up the paper. Stick to your outline but be willing to include information that comes up as you are writing. Avoid making general statements and rambling. Often teachers will have several points and/or facts that they want to see in the answer. Try to get them in. This shows that you know your stuff.

✦ TIP #152
Paragraph often.

Paragraphing is an aid to the reader. It groups information in convenient little chunks of similar material about the same subject. Try reading an unparagraphed page in a book and you will understand how important paragraphing is. A good guide of when to begin a new paragraph would be to paragraph with each major division of your outline. Be sure to leave some additional space between essays and to title each essay, indicating which question you are writing about.

✦ TIP 153
Use transitional words.

Transitional words and expressions help you get gracefully from one point to another. They show that you are controlling the flow and organization of your answer (and teachers love them). Transitions are words such as *therefore*, *after that*, *consequently* (this one is really impressive), and *finally*. Transitions show relationships, such as time and cause and effect, between different ideas that you are writing about.

✦ TIP #154
Proofread your paper when you have finished writing.

When you have finished writing your answers, save a little time to carefully re-read your essays. If possible, do it out loud, or at least mouth the words. This is when you do your editing. Check your mechanics, sentence structure, grammar, punctuation and spelling. Here is where you should catch dumb errors.

If you feel the need to make errors, make sophisticated ones. Don't make simple mistakes, like transposing words in a sentence. If you recall additional information that you want to add, do it in the margin.

✦ TIP #155
Running out of time?

If you are running short on time, make sure you have outlined your answer. Add more detail to the outline. That way your teacher can see what you would have written and possibly give you at least partial credit.

SOME ADDITIONAL ADVICE ON HOW TO TAKE MIXED, OBJECTIVE-SUBJECTIVE TESTS

✦ TIP #156
Check out the whole test first.

Sometimes essay questions are included at the end of mixed-question tests. Look over the entire test and read the essay questions carefully before you attempt to answer anything. This way you will know what you are up against and you won't be surprised later to discover a part of the test that you didn't know existed. Be sure to check the back of the test paper. (Sometimes teachers "hide" questions there!)

✦ TIP #157
It's just as important to budget your time on mixed question tests.

If it is a mixed objective-subjective test, figure out how much time to devote to each section. Do the easy objective questions first, then the ones you must guess at before proceeding to the essay section. Budget your time for the essay questions independently of the rest of the test, if there is one. Remember to allow about 10% of the time to plan your answers and about 10% to review and edit your answers.

✦ TIP #158
Afterwards...

Again, when you get your paper back, be sure that you understand what you did right and what needs improvement.

CHAPTER 11

A BRIEF ONE FOR PARENTS K-6

WHAT CAN I DO IN K-6?

We, as parents, all want our kids to be the smartest, most talented and best looking, and sometimes we may tend to push (or at least nudge) our kids in the direction and at the pace we would like to see. Even though this book is intended for students in grade seven and up, there is no invisible line between grade six and grade seven. Some of these techniques can be introduced earlier than seventh grade, but it is up to you to determine how much can be absorbed by your students. Sometimes you will even have to wait for your seventh grader to be ready for some of them.

Maturing and growing up is a gradual process, and it's difficult to tell sometimes just which study skills a child can learn at any given age. The absolute best thing you as a parent of K-6 children can do is to allow them to be children. Don't be too concerned with what study skills are being learned, how well they can study or how much they are learning. If your child is healthy and normal, chill out. Let them enjoy childhood. They will develop to the point where they can learn study skills.

Having said that, here is my advice on what you can do for your children in K-6. What is most important for K-6 children to learn, besides how to be kids? I think it's attitude. Children should enjoy their lives, and the world around them should be a source of wonder to be explored and understood. They should feel secure, loved and wanted. They shouldn't have to deal with stress, worry or anxiety any more than necessary. They should enjoy learning and discovery and form a positive attitude toward it.

You know your children better than anyone else. Observe how they learn. I wouldn't be obsessive about it, but notice if they are visual, auditory or tactile learners. Do they exhibit any special areas of intelligence? If you can determine this, then play to that strength—but don't play too hard.

Be patient and teach what students can learn. In second grade, my granddaughter, Jordan, had a very difficult time with reading, so much so that it frustrated both her and her mother. With time, and a little maturity, the problem rectified itself. Today she reads on or above grade level, and she loves to read. What was the problem? She just wasn't ready for it yet.

First graders aren't going to be setting goals like an eleventh grader, but you can teach them what goals are and help them set little ones.

Kids love to memorize rhymes and jingles. They love to play with sounds. It is fun for them—if you make it fun. Look at what Dr. Seuss did.

Teach them what good TV is. Better yet, model it for them. You can't expect children to watch good TV if the parents don't. Children learn what they see, and you are (or should be) the most important influence on them. When I started my teaching career, an old veteran told me that no matter what I did in front of a class, I was teaching. If I goofed off and wasted time, that's what I was teaching my students, that it was OK to goof off and waste time. When we have children we all become teachers by default–24 hours a day.

Play games with your K-6 children. Play physical games and mental games. Tag, baseball, and backyard badminton–these are all beneficial for your kids. Sometimes I think that kids are too regimented today and expected to join an organized team sport–or sports. What's wrong with just playing some pick-up baseball games–like whenever? Children don't have to have every minute of their day organized. Sometimes it's OK to just play in the dirt.

Teach them how to play checkers and maybe chess. Kids love a challenge and naturally take to games. Lots of kids' games are fun and educational for them.

Teach them to use all their senses. Go for a walk in the woods and ask them what they hear, smell and feel. Let them suck the nectar from a honeysuckle and smell the leaves of a walnut tree–or whatever grows where you live. Try to make things meaningful for them.

As they start writing entire compositions, you may try to introduce some pre-writing techniques. Not all of them, just some that may help them.

As you gradually try to introduce skills, if they aren't ready for it yet, stop. You can try all these things for your K-6 children, but the best thing you can do for them is to love them. Your children are the most precious gifts that God has given to you. They are the focal point of your life. Our lives before children lead up to them. And after they have left home, we look back on those times as the most meaningful of our lives. The best thing we can do with our lives is to train our children well before we send them out to conquer the world. If you love them, you will lead them.

FOR FURTHER STUDY

For those of you who would like to delve deeper into learning concepts, the following go into much more detail than the scope of this book encompasses.

101 Ways to Improve Your Memory: Games, Tricks, Strategies. New York: Readers Digest, 2005.

Adams, Beverly L. and others. *Home School, High School, & Beyond: A Time Management, Career Exploration, Organizational & Study Skills Course,* 4th ed. New York: Castlemoyle Books,1999.

Brainard, Lee Wherry and Ricki Wingardner. *10 Secrets to Mastering Any High School Test,* 2nd ed. New York: Learning Express, 2003.

Carneigie, Dale. *How to Develop Self-Confidence and Influence People by Public Speaking.* New York: Pocket books, 1956.

Culter, Wade E. *Triple Your Reading Speed,* 4th ed. New York: Pocket Books, 2003.

Donald, R.B. and others. *Writing Clear Essays,* 3rd ed. Upper Saddle River, NJ: Simon and Schuster, 1996.

Ebbinghaus, Hermann. *Memory: A Contribution to Experimental Psychology* (1885). Trans. Henry A. Ruger & Clara E. Bussenius. New York: Teachers College, Columbia University,1913.

Gardner, Howard. *Frames of Mind: The theory of multiple intelligences.* New York: Basic Books, 1993.

Hagwood, Scott. *Memory Power: You Can Develop A Great Memory–America's Grand Master Shows You How.* New York: Free Press, 2005.

James, Art and Dennis Katz. *Effective Listening Skills.* New York: McGraw Hill.

Mandino, Og. *The Greatest Salesman in the World.* Hollywood, FL: Frederick Fell, 1968.

McClain, Molly and Jacqueline D. Roth. *Schaum's Quick Guide to Writing Great Essays.* New York: McGraw-Hill, 1998.

McPherson, Fiona. *The Memory Key: Unlock the Secrets to Remembering.* Franklin Lakes, NY: Career Press, 2000.